The ELM PARK STORY

From Garden City to London Suburb

By

Chris Hipperson, Simon Donoghue and Ingrid Brandon .

Havering
LONDON BOROUGH

Published by

London Borough of Havering Library Service

Printed and bound in Great Britain by
The Lavenham Press Limited
Lavenham, Suffolk

ELM PARK

ELM PARK
ROMFORD

The New
HOME
CENTRE

STAIN

THE COMPLETE COUNTRY H
Planned & built by
RICHARD COSTAIN
COSTAIN HOUSE, UPPER WOBURN PL
LONDON W.C.1.

OFFI

ESTATE

ELM PARK
The New
HOME
CENTRE

PICTORIAL
TO SHOW THE FACTS — TO TELL THE TRU
Published by Richard Costain Ltd. House Builders, &c

OLD ENGLAND'S BROAD ACRES
HER BEST HOMEL

Blackwall
Tunnel
Canning Twn
Stn (LNER)
Balsam
Street
Greengate
Street
Green Street
Barking Rd
East Ham
Town Hall
Burges
Road
Barking
Broadway
Barking
Westbury H
Ripple Rd
The Harrow
Cemetery Gts
Ripple Rd
Rippleside
Ship & Shvl
Gale
Street
Dagenham
Chequers I
New Road
Mission H
South
Street

Balsam
S
Greengate
S
Green St
Barking
Rd
East Ham
Town Hall
Burges
Road
Barking
Broadway
Barking
Westbury H
Ripple Rd
The Harrow
Cemetery Gts
Ripple Rd
Rippleside
Ship & Shvl
Gale
Street
Dagenham
Chequers I
Dagenham
Church Elm
New Road
Mission H
South
Street
Rainham
Clock Tow

L. G. O. CO. LTD. & ASSOCIATED COS. Ltd

SERVICE 122 & 2

A

D

Contents

ELM PARK : AN INTRODUCTION

Elm Park is less than 15 miles from the busy, bustling centre of London but it was largely peaceful open countryside until just over three quarters of a century ago when the arrival of a large housing development and the Tube totally transformed the area. The Elm Park Garden City and the new District Line railway station were officially opened in May 1935 by the Minister of Health, Sir Hilton Young MP. The brand new estate of 7,000 proposed new homes was to be built on 600 acres of land at a cost of £3,500,000 by Richard Costain Limited after the purchase of the Elm Farm in 1933.

This book traces the origins of Elm Park and explores the history of the manors and farms, which predated the modern housing estate. With memorable photographs and moving personal recollections from residents past and present, Elm Park's unique and absorbing story is vividly brought to life.

On the eve of its 75th anniversary a new chapter in Elm Park's history has already begun with an annual Fiesta, a series of collectable postage stamps and the opening of London's first low carbon library. The present is certainly full of promise but, as the past of this highly individual and distinctive district unfolds, it reveals a rich oral history and a remarkable heritage.

The very idea of Elm Park as a city may seem absurd today, but in the 1930s the ideals of the Garden City movement were influential and fashionably forward-thinking. The Garden City Association was formed in May 1900 by prominent urban planner Sir Ebeneezer Howard, who had Utopian ideas for planned developments of self-contained communities in a green setting, balancing the needs of housing, industry and agriculture.

Letchworth Garden City and Welwyn Garden City were founded on Howard's ideas and smaller scale suburban developments soon followed; notably Hampstead Garden Suburb and in Havering, the Gidea Park Exhibition Estate of 1911. Milton Keynes became the last and largest Garden City but the imaginative concept lived on and Walt Disney used elements of Howard's ideas in his design for EPCOT (Experimental Prototype Community of Tomorrow) in Florida. Attaching the term 'Garden Suburb' or 'Garden City' to almost any new housing development became part of the sales pitch. Upminster was sold as a garden suburb, though there was little attempt to plan anything beyond the individual houses. Locally it could be argued that the London County Council Harold Hill estate built after the Second World War was among the closest to the ideals of the Garden City movement.

But the vision of an independent and individual way of living was in some ways best realised in Elm Park Garden City. Of course, Elm Park is certainly no city, nor was it ever intended to be. Unlike much of the inter War development of London suburbs it was carefully planned with a mixed range of family homes and great attention was paid to the transport, shopping and leisure needs of the new residents. In these respects the builders Costain learned vitally important lessons from the Garden City movement. The pioneering residents who first arrived to live in Elm Park certainly created vibrant gardens in their new suburb of London. In other respects Elm Park is at odds with Sir Ebeneezer's ideals. There was no planned industrial area; the agricultural land around the estate soon disappeared and housing was built at a higher density than the Council's own plans allowed for.

At the same time Elm Park was brilliantly marketed and Costain offered something, which the garden suburbs elsewhere did not: home ownership for many people who until then had no prospect of buying a house. Good family homes were built and a real sense of community, which happily still exists, was created in those early years. The houses themselves have stood the test of time, retaining much of their original character but proving flexible for sympathetic extensions and loft conversions.

The Second World War prevented Costain from completing what they had started. A desperate shortage of housing and building materials, together with a new political landscape altered priorities. It would be interesting to know how Elm Park would have looked if the War hadn't intervened.

Front cover: The front cover design is based on the Coronation Arcadia brochure produced by Costain in 1937. The striking painting of the house and car is by Jackson Burton.

Back cover: The award winning low carbon Elm Park Library

FOREWORD AND ACKNOWLEDGEMENTS

In 1995, when Chris Hipperson was Branch Librarian at Elm Park Library, she and the Library staff researched and presented an exhibition to celebrate 60 years of Elm Park. **The Elm Park Story: an exhibition to celebrate the diamond anniversary of the Elm Park Garden City** generated huge interest and further exhibitions followed; **Elm Park Library's 40th Birthday, Shops and Shopping**, **On the street where you live** and in 2000 **Millennium time capsule.** Enormous interest built up and there were many requests to 'put it all in a book.'

In 2008, Elm Park's long-serving 'temporary' library was demolished. It was replaced by a new, award-winning library for the 21st Century, which was officially opened on Monday 8th June 2009.

Ingrid Brandon, a member of the Elm Park Regeneration Partnership, thought it would be a great idea to celebrate the new library with a book, which told the history of Elm Park.

This volume, which has grown from that suggestion, is based on the Elm Park Library exhibitions of the 1990's and the memories of many local residents which were then collected by the library staff. Material from the London Borough of Havering Local Studies Library has been added as well as much new research, interviews, photographs and specially written articles to tell **The Elm Park Story: From Garden City to London Suburb**

Thanks and acknowledgements

Many local residents have been generous in sharing their memories, photographs and documents for this book.
Particular thanks are due to:
Martin Hipperson who worked on photographs and assisted with research. **Brian Cornwell** who, apart from providing reminiscences of wartime and writing the section about the Church of St Nicholas, also provided additional information and a number of unique illustrations. **Jeremy Wilkes** who provided a history of the Elm Park Horticultural Guild. **Kes Cole** who took many of the modern photographs. **Stafford Hildred** for editorial assistance. **Elm Park Library Staff** particularly between 1995 and 2000 who did so much to make the library exhibitions a great success.
Staff of the Havering Central Reference Library; particularly **Julie Johns** and **Jane Finnett** who have assisted with research and practical assistance for this book and in support of the Elm Park Library exhibitions.
And finally, our grateful thanks to all at Lavenham Press, especially **David Tokeley** creative designer, for his patience and skill in producing an excellent design and layout of this book.

We thank all those who have contributed to this book including the following individuals and organisations:

Edna Bono	Sheila Fry	Rod Moffatt
Brentwood News	Alan Fulcher	Glenn Morgan
Anne Clements	Ken Gibson	Howard Moss
Ken Coe	Freda Gill	Peter Moss
Pat Coe	Les Graves	Ethel Page
Vera Cornwell	Jean Hancock	Eileen Popkin
Mrs Crouch	Alan Hassell	Del Ramsey
Malcolm Cullen	Doris Hedley	Ian Rice
Ken Daley	Jeff Hills	Ena Risby
Linda Daley	Jack Hoepelman	Ron Sampson
Tom Daley	Margaret Hoepelman	Joan Shoush
Mavis Darby	Evelyn Holloway	Sue Smith
Ray Dempsey	Ian Hunt	Patricia Snelling
Rita Demspey	Adrian Janes	Norman Sparrow
Ken Elliott	Joan Leary	Dorothy Stimpson
Win Eshelby	Elsie Leeder	Fred Thorogood
Ted Exall	George Leeder	Mike Trevaillon
M.A. Farmer	Peter Lines	Roy Turnbull
Betty Foster	Christine Malby	George Vellacott
Fr. Stewart Foster, Diocesan Archivist and Historian of Brentwood Diocese	Terry Malby	Christine White
	Mrs McCarthy	Eileen Wilson
	Joan McGovern	Graham Wilson
Jean Franklin	Pauline Medley	Patrick Wynne

Information has been gathered over a period of years and many unnamed contributors have helped with research, confirmed facts or provided anecdotes. We are very grateful for all the assistance we have had and apologise for any name missed from the list above.

This book is dedicated to all the residents of Elm Park, past and present. We hope you enjoy reading your story:

Chris Hipperson
Simon Donoghue
Ingrid Brandon
2009

EARLY HISTORY

Elm Park is situated on land created during the Ice Ages between 10,000 and 500,000 years ago. The whole of the Hornchurch district down to the River Thames stands on gravel terraces formed as the river was forced south. Largely as a result of continuing gravel extraction, evidence of habitation has been uncovered which gives an impression of previous life in this area.

Although there has been little archaeological investigation of sites in Elm Park, excavations of the former residential home, Maybank Lodge in Maybank Avenue, indicated evidence of an Iron Age and an early mediaeval settlement. At the southern end of Elm Park, in Silverdale Drive, a Roman kiln was identified. There is also a suggestion that a Roman Road once ran between London and Bradwell in Essex alongside the route of the District Line between Elm Park and Hornchurch. Evidence to the east, west and south suggests the land at Elm Park has been occupied for thousands of years. Old Stone Age tools were found at nearby Scotts and Albyns Farm. Further east, at Berwick Ponds, ancient tools and part of an elephant's tooth were found.

As woodland was cleared small settlements were established and mixed farming was introduced. Stone Age flints, tools and pottery have been found in Rainham as well as ritual monuments or henge. Gravel extraction in what is now part of Hornchurch Country Park revealed prehistoric flints and pottery as well as Roman pottery and coins. Excavation of sites near Rainham Road revealed a Late Bronze

1928 discovery of a Roman coffin at South Hornchurch.

Age settlement with field systems, enclosures, post structures, pits, hearths and cremation burials, dating to 9th-8th centuries BC. A Late Bronze Age round house was found in South Hornchurch and small Iron Age settlements have been recorded at Moor Hall Farm and Hunts Hill Farm, Rainham.

In 1928, dramatic evidence of Roman occupation in the area was found during house building near the junction of Frederick Road and Manser Road. A stone coffin from the Third Century A.D. containing two bodies was uncovered. The bodies had been laid head to foot, but the remains disintegrated when the casket was opened. This burial site had, according to an eyewitness who spoke to the local historian Frank Lewis years later, been surrounded by 'little glass jars with bits of bone' which had been 'tossed aside' and it is likely this was a long established burial site predating Roman Christianity. The Roman town of Durolitum is thought to have been in Romford and in addition to finds already referred to, Roman wells were found on the LESSA sports ground off Cherry Tree Lane and at Moor Hall Farm. Evidence that new foods, like carrots, coriander and celery were introduced to this country by the Romans, was found in seeds discovered in this neighbourhood and the head of a honeybee was found at Moor Hall Farm.

By the end of the Fifth Century most of Eastern England was under Anglo-Saxon rule and 100 years later the London region was a province of an East Saxon kingdom. An important group of Sixth Century pagan Saxon burials found at Gerpins Pit included two rare glass drinking horns, spears, shield bosses and gold jewellery.

The Saxons established a palace at Havering-atte-Bower in the Seventh century that lasted until the 17th Century and the Domesday Book of 1086 records that **Harold held Havering in 1066 as one Manor**. Harold's predecessor, King Edward the Confessor, often held his court at Havering and there are a number of legends associating Edward with Havering.

One of two Anglo-Saxon glass drinking horns found at Gerpins

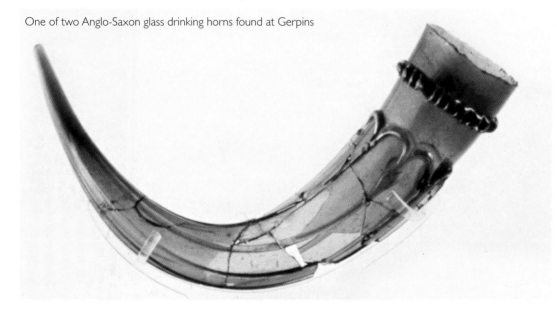

THE ROYAL MANOR OF HAVERING AND ELM PARK'S MANORS

Much of Elm Park's history is associated with that of the Royal Manor of Havering, the Royal Liberty of Havering-atte-Bower, from its creation in 1465, and the Parish of Hornchurch, the ecclesiastical centre of the Royal Manor and Liberty whose boundaries it shared.

Within the Manor of Havering there were several tenements or manors. Modern Elm Park was built mainly on land which was formerly part of the manor of **Maylards Green and Wybridge**, two parts of the same estate divided by what is shown as Bowles Brook in 1777 (earlier Bollesbroke) and farms from **Suttons Manor**; Elm Farm and Uphavering Farm. The other significant manor in the area was **Bretons** though only a small portion of this became part of the original Elm Park estate.

Maylards is thought to derive from the Maylor or Maylers family name, which is found among the witnesses to several documents associated with Hornchurch Priory in the 13th and 14th centuries, such John le Meylur (1260-62). The corruption to Maylands Green dates from the 19th Century. Reaney's **Place Names of Essex** suggests that Wybridge may represent a lost name for the Beam River. The name derives from the family of Wybregge c1233/Wibregge 1250/1 and it is possible there is an ownership link with Whybridge a little further south.

Owners of the manor included the judge Sir Anthony Browne who founded Brentwood School in 1558. Sir Anthony died in 1567 at Weald Hall and later that year his wife conveyed the manor of Maylerds, alias Maylard Greene and Wybridges, to Robert Charnock and William Fawkener. At that time the manor contained:

> 2 messauges, 3 tofts, 3 cottages, 3 dovehouses, 3 gardens, 3 orchards, 100 acres of arable, 30 acres of meadow, 300 acres of pasture and 10 acres of wood

Wybridge was divided from Maylards after this date and William Ayloffe of Bretons owned Wybridge until his death in 1627. In 1657 William Thorowgood was the owner.

Maylards had passed to Sir James Rushout (Bt.) by 1659. His son, also Sir James, succeeded him. The younger Sir James died in 1711, without marrying, and Maylards went to his sister Elizabeth, wife of Sir Paulet St. John of Dogmersfield in Hampshire. When she died without issue, Maylards was sold to John Bamber MD and the manor descended with the Bifrons estate in Barking to the Gascoynes and then to the Gascoyne-Cecils – the Marquesses of Salisbury.

When John Bamber died in 1799 Wybridge had returned to the Maylards estate and was inherited by Bamber Gascoyne.

Suttons manor was granted to Hornchurch Priory by Henry II around 1158. The name is thought to derive from an early owner of the manor and this is first recorded in 1257. In mediaeval times the Suttons estate extended south from Hornchurch to Dovers Corner and was bounded in the east by the River Ingrebourne and to the west by Abbs Cross Lane.

Bretons in Upper Rainham Road is Palladian style farmhouse, rebuilt around 1740 on the ruins of a Tudor house. This Grade II listed building was drawn by Alfred Bennett Bamford in 1899

In 1391 on the dissolution of the priory William of Wykeham, Bishop of Winchester, purchased the Hornchurch Priory estates to endow New College, Oxford. The church owned Suttons, Hornchurch Hall and various estates elsewhere in the parish. In 1663, New College owned 840 acres of land in Hornchurch; by 1849 this had risen to 930 acres, of which 406 acres was the Suttons estate.

The name **Bretons** has been traced through various spellings, Breteyness (1517), Bretouns (1359) and probably originated with Radulphus Briton (1177), an association lasting through to the 14th Century. Sir Richard Arundel held the manor along with Baldwins and Mardyke when he made his will in 1417 before joining the army of Henry V in France. In 1476 Thomas Scargill of Bretons made a request in his will for the building of a steeple at St Andrews Church, Hornchurch, which is still a significant local landmark today. In 1501 the house came into the possession of the Ayloffe family who remained for 150 years and built a new house on the site. Sir Benjamin Ayloffe , a prominent royalist during the Civil War, had to sell Bretons to meet the costs imposed on him by Parliament. The buyer was John Winniffe who sold Bretons to John Austen. Austen's son, also John, held the manor in 1720.

By 1742, the owner of Bretons was John Hopkins who rebuilt the house. Hopkins, who also held Redden Court in Harold Wood, was a renowned miser and money lender, commonly known as Vulture Hopkins, even inspiring Alexander Pope to the lines:

> **When Hopkins dies a thousand lights attend**
> **The wretch who living saved a candle's end.**

His death in 1722 saw the two manors passed to John Dare and these manors descended together until parts of the estate were sold in 1858. Bretons was eventually sold to the Romford Local Board for use as a sewage farm, which opened in 1869 and closed in 1969.

INTO THE 19TH CENTURY – A FARMING COMMUNITY

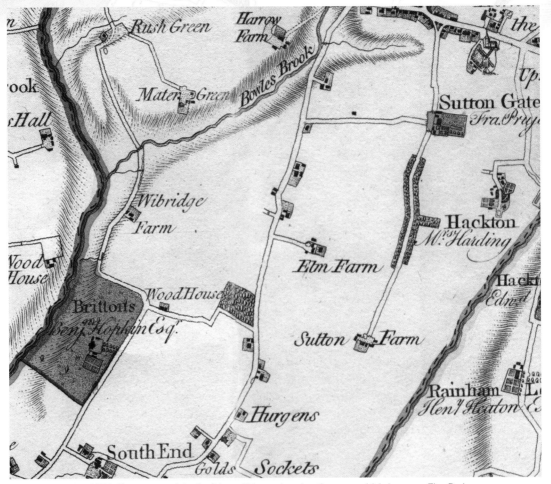

Extract from the 1977 Chapman and Andre Map of Essex showing the area which became Elm Park

Chapman and Andre's map of Essex, published in 1777, shows roads and farms familiar to the modern traveller. Maylands is Mater Green alongside Harrow Farm and Wibridge Farm. Wood House illustrates the origin of Wood Lane which then, as now, links Rainham Road to the South End Road. Bretons is Brittons and is shown as a substantial estate owned by Benjamin Hopkins. Also shown are Elm Farm, Sutton Farm, Hurgens which became Algores and Sockets which remains as Albyns Farm.

A more detailed picture of the people in the Elm Park landscape and some idea of what they were doing is available from the 1812 Hornchurch Parish Map and a corresponding apportionment book detailing ownership of the fields shown on the map.

Wybridge or Weybridge was possessed by Bamber Gascoyne and the size of the farm was 276 acres 2 rods and 4 perches. There are two homesteads as well as a cottage and garden. The main Wybridge house is in a cluster of 10 buildings next to the Rainham Road. Maylards consisted of 168a 0r 8p. Gascoyne also owned Havering Well Farm to the north west and Argents Farm off South End Road.

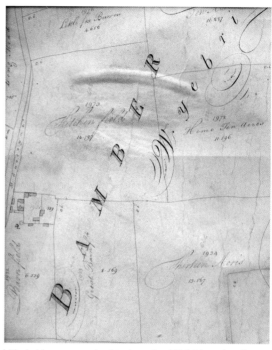

No. on Plan	Description	Homestd a. r. p	Arable a. r. p	Mea &c. a. r. p	Wood a. r. p
435	Three Acres		3 1 17		
438	Meadow			1 1 34	
439	Meadow			1 1 18	
440	Garden	. 1 32			
441	Homestead	. 3 22			
442	Barn Field			6 2 6	
443	Great Barn Field		8 2 14		
444	Thirteen Acres		13 2 16		
445	Four Acres		4 1 8		
473	Six Acres		6 3 22		
474	Homestead	1 1 15			
475	Home Field		3 . 7		
479	Hull Tree Field		9 1 28		
480	Long Six Acres		6 2 24		
481	Three Acres		3 3 18		
482	Home Ten Acres		11 2 15		
	Carr. forw	2 2 29	71 1 9	9 1 18	

Detail from book accompanying the 1812 Hornchurch Parish Map showing Bamber Gascoyne's ownership of *Weybridge*

Wyebridge manor depicted on the 1812 Hornchurch Parish Map

New College, Oxford owned Sutton Farm, and various other portions of land some of which was leased to others. Esmead Edridge farmed over 134 acres of land including Elm Farm, which has an orchard and 59 acres of arable land. Uphavering Farm is shown on the 1812 map, farmed by John Finch Holding. Though Holding is the only name on the map, George Rickards is also named in the book. George Holding Rickards, purchased Uphavering and Elm Farm from New College in 1871. Baileys sits between Uphavering and Elm Farm.

Towards South Hornchurch, Mary Hills owned Albins Farm, which included osiers (willow trees), a well field and another field known as sand pit field. George Adam Askew held land shown as Adgores, as well as a Smith's Shop, probably one of several buildings he possessed in Abbs Cross Lane. Joseph

Elm Farm 1812

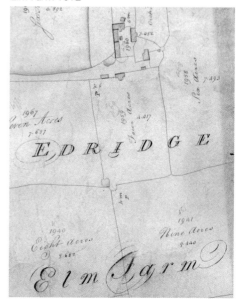

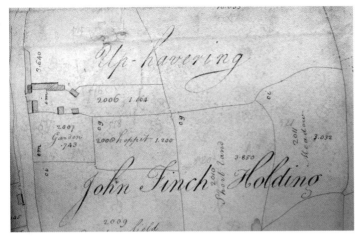

Uphavering Farm 1812

Elms Uphavering and Bayleys 1870

Osborn had land just south of Adgores, though his largest holding was the land around modern day Osborne Road in Hornchurch where he grew lilies.

Dunningford Farm was owned by William Hilton. The land was mostly south of Wood Lane though the 1812 map shows some fields north of Wood Lane next to the Rainham Road. The Brittains estate across Rainham Road also extended north across Wood Lane. Other landowners within Elm Park included New College, Berchett Wheeler of Harrow Farm and Christopher Tyler of Whybridge Manor (alias Rands Manor) in South Hornchurch, who had Wood Fields in Elm Park.

The Hornchurch Parish Tithe Map of 1849 shows a similar landscape, though some names are different. Elm Farm is shown as Newells Farm, Uphavering is Upper Havering Farm and Baileys Farm seems to have more substantial buildings than in 1812. Otherwise there is no real evidence of further building along the main roads. The manors are shown as the substantial farms they had been for many years, Brittains Farm, Wyebridge Farm and Maylards Green Farm.

Trade directories occasionally add detail but they can be inconsistent and sometimes include only substantial landowners or significant traders. White's Directory of Essex 1848 lists John Massu Stanley at Malins Green and Anthony Vince at Whybridge though the location of most traders isn't specified. Under the heading FARMERS in 1863, White's Directory of Essex shows John Henry Paine at Up-Havering and Anthony Vince still at Wyebridge. Nearby Albyns and Scotts is farmed by Mary and William Bonnett, a family still associated with agriculture in Havering in the 21st Century. Kelly's Directory of 1878 identifies James Fraser as a farmer and auctioneer at Malins Green, while Mr Vince remains at Wyebridge Farm.

Outside the Good Intent at the end of the nineteenth century

The Good Intent public house also appears in this directory with George Oliver as landlord. The pub is thought to date back beyond 1818, though originally it was a beerhouse operating from a cottage. Subsequent directories show little change but in the 1886 Kelly's Directory the arrival of the railways is noted:

> **HORNCHURCH is a village and parish with a station on the new branch of the London, Tilbury and Southend railway, pleasantly situated on the road from Romford to Upminster and within the liberty of Havering-atte-Bower.**

Although the landscape remained agricultural, the new railway line and stations opened at Hornchurch and Upminster in 1885 had an enormous and immediate impact. As can be seen on the 1897 Ordnance Survey map, the line cut straight through Wyebridge, Uphavering Farm and Elms Farm and Baileys disappeared completely taking with it the homes of farm labourers. There were long term consequences too. Within 50 years the farms were gone and the location of the railway line was crucial to the creation and positioning of the Elm Park Estate.

Perhaps the richest source of information about the residents of this area is the Census which has taken place every 10 years since 1801, with individual names recorded from 1841. There was no Census in 1941 due to the War though a mini

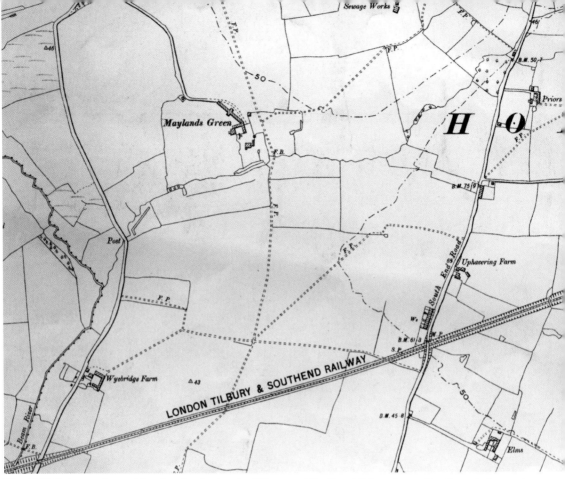

The 1897 Ordnance Survey Map showing the London, Tilbury and Southend Railway line cutting through the rural landscape.

census to issue identity cards did take place in September 1939. The Census is important because it tells us about everybody in the locality, not just the owners of land.

In 1871 for example, most people living in the Elm Park area were agricultural labourers, such as William Raiment who lived with his wife Sarah, their three children and a nephew, also working as an agricultural labourer, at Wood House in Wood Lane.

There is detailed information about the farms in the district. At Wyebridge Farm, Anthony Vince was living with his sister Elizabeth Cain and his two daughters. Emma Grimwood was visiting and Vince employed a domestic servant. The number of people employed on this 170 acre farm is detailed on the Census; 18 men, one boy and six women. Elm Farm was farmed by Brooks Gooch. He was, like many people in the area, originally from Suffolk. In 1871 the farm stretched over 400 acres and employed 30 men, 20 women and 12 boys. Not only are there two domestic servants, but a governess, too. Gooch's groom George Rawlingson, in the neighbouring Elm Cottage, was also from Suffolk.

Other trades in Elm Park and South Hornchurch included a manure manufacturer; Henry Nobbs at Uphavering farm, a blacksmith, butcher, farm bailiff, a Chelsea pensioner; Simon Swan, a 69 year old, living in Clay Cottages, a shepherd, carpenter, bricklayer and wheelwright. The beershop was the Good Intent along South End Road with George Oliver as landlord. In the cottage next door are the Pamments, a family who later took over running the Good Intent.

Most residents had been born locally at either Hornchurch, Romford, Rainham, Cranham, or South Ockendon. However there was a significant influx of farmworkers from Suffolk with others coming from Wiltshire, Bedfordshire, Suffolk, Bristol and Ireland.

A glimpse of the social life in the area is offered in this extract from the St Andrew's Parish Magazine of May 1894 describing a lantern slideshow at the South Hornchurch chapel by Mr and Mrs Hussey of Uphavering Farm. The lantern slides of Hornchurch in the snow would be fascinating to see now!

SOUTH HORNCHURCH.

A very pleasing, instructive, and interesting free Lantern Entertainment entitled "The Home of Our Queen at Windsor" (photograph taken at the time of the Jubilee Celebration in 1887, by special permission of Her Majesty), followed by a Series of Slides of Hornchurch under Snow, January 8th, 1894, with descriptive lecture, was kindly given by Mr. and Mrs. Hussey, Uphavering, to a crowded audience in South Hornchurch School, April 16th, the chair being taken by C. O. May, Esq., of Sutton's Gate.

Change was slow in this part of Hornchurch but there was gradual development along Abbs Cross Lane and South End Road, mainly with farm workers cottages. Hornchurch parish opened a mission church, and Mrs. Skeale's Church infants school also began, in 1864. In the 1890 Kelly's Directory, Samuel John Curtis appears as a shopkeeper in Wood Lane, perhaps a sign of a growing and changing population.

ELM PARK IN THE EARLY 20TH CENTURY

SOUTH HORNCHURCH.

Biddick James, Upper Havering house
Goss Edward
Pyner John James, Wood lane
Softly William George, Ford lodge

COMMERCIAL.

Blows James, farmer, Weybridge (letters through Rainham, Essex)
Bonnett Dick, farmer, Grove farm
Bonnett Samuel, farmer, Albyns farm
Cotton William, shopkeeper
Cutler William, shopkeeper
Fell C. & Son, shopkeepers
Gay Alfred, farmer, Maylands Green
Gay William John, farmer
Gentry James, reed layer
Jones Joseph, farmer, Mardyke farm
Pamment Margaret (Miss), beer retlr
Phillips Eliza (Mrs.), shopkeeper
Polley James, farm bailiff to W. Vellacott, Elm farm
Poupart John, farmer, Dovers
Reed Samuel G. Cherry Tree P.H
Romford Rural District Council Sewage Farm (Chas. A. Hall, mgr)
Romford Urban Dist. Council Sewage Farm (William Strachan, manager)
Stone Alfred, farmer, Princes farm
Thorogood Samuel, farmer
Turpin Fredk. Wm. farmer, Ford frm
Ward Henry, shopkeeper
Winmill Edwd. farmer, Weybridge frm
Wright William, shopkeeper

Kelly's Directory listing for South Hornchurch 1910

Residents of Elm Park can find on the deeds of their homes names that existed before the estate was built; Albyn, Argent, Brittons, Elm, Dunningford, Halls, Uphavering, or Wyebridge Farms. These names and the farms have, as we have seen, a long history. It is interesting to see a snapshot of the area in the 1910 Kelly's Directory. As the population of the Hornchurch Parish grew the commercial directories such as Kelly's began to list the different parts of the parish separately. Historically much of Elm Park was in the South End of the Hornchurch Parish and this farming community is well illustrated here.

From the beginning of the 20th Century and especially after the First World War changes in Hornchurch occurred rapidly. Many farms and large estates were sold off for housing. Romford Rural District Council had erected council houses in Abbs Cross Lane and the population was expanding and changing. The arrival of the railways made Hornchurch and the neighbouring towns and villages easily accessible from London and property developers quickly built over the farmlands that had sustained the local economy for centuries.

The 1920s directories show a wider range of occupations and the building of New Road dividing South Hornchurch from Rainham brought motor mechanics, fried fish shops, furniture dealers and other new retailers. In 1929 we also find another symptom of the massive surge in building between the two World Wars. Edward Winmill, had become the proprietor of Wyebridge Sand and Ballast Pits, Rainham Road. Further along Rainham Road is the River Rom Sand and Gravel Pits and at Algores Farm there is James Newman, Haulage Contractor.

Mr Gower of Priors Farm, which was just north of Uphavering Farm off Abbs Cross Lane, provides a rare view of a domestic interior in the early twentieth century.

The newly reopened aerodrome on Suttons Farm, destined to play such a significant role in the Battle of Britain and the life of the soon to arrive residents of Elm Park, is also listed:

> Royal Air Force 111 (F) Squadron; Squadron Leader F O Soden DFC commanding officer H W Banks, steward Telephone Numbers Rainham 142 & 143.

ELM FARM

As the story of Elm Park is about to leave behind the agricultural world of centuries we are fortunate to have the recorded memories of **George Vellacott** of Elm Farm and of **Fred Thorogood** the son of Fred Thorogood the farm's steward from 1916, which brilliantly capture life before the Elm Park estate was built.

George Vellacott recalled:

> Elm Farm was part of the Manor of Suttons and was owned by New College, Oxford. They were absentee landlords, which

meant that tenant farmers paid rent to the college. The farm was sold to George Rickards together with Uphavering Farm and Wood Lane Field. Both the farms still had tenant farmers who paid rent. When Mr Rickards died, ownership passed to his niece Eleanor and then to her son Arthur Rickards. In 1885 some of the land was sold to the London Tilbury and Southend Railway (LTSR).

In 1913 the land was sold again and Walter Vellacott became the new owner of Elm Farm. The old farmhouse stood off the South End Road, just south of the railway line, surrounded by an orchard. There were two huge pear trees, cherry trees, and rows of Cox's Orange Pippin trees. The road, Farm Way, is built over the quarter mile track to the house. This track often became very muddy in winter and the horses found it hard to negotiate. There were stables for the horses, a big barn, bunching sheds where crops were boxed for market and behind the shed was an old clay pug house where bricks were made. There was a horse pond where the horses would come to drink at meal times. In the evenings they would wade into the water thigh high, shaded by huge old horse chestnut trees. At the beginning of the 20th Century the farm employed 15 or more men. Wages were low: a man earned two pounds a week if he was lucky. If he earned three pounds by doing piece-work he thought that he'd done tremendously well. In those days the horses did a lot of the hard work on the farm.

The horsemen at the Elm Farm were skilled men. They could 'drill within an inch'. No tractor man would attempt to plant so accurately. Everything used to work to a plan. It was the traditional skills of centuries handed down. Crops were grown in rotation to enrich the soil. The horses did not cost very much to keep because the farm grew oats and hay and bedding straw. Crops were packed in bushel boxes. Harry Bixsby and his wife could fill a hundred cabbage boxes before breakfast. Bert Bowlford could

Elm Farm 1923

bunch a hundred dozen onions a day without thinking about it. In those days it wasn't string or rubber bands used for tying but willow tie rods, some of which were grown on the farm. The rest were bought from a firm up near the market, bushel bags were bought by the thousand from a firm called Andrews.

Mr Thorogood's sketch map showing the planting of crops at Elm Farm. N.B. The labelling of the South End Road as Rainham Road is not a mistake; Census Surveys also list properties in this road in the same way.

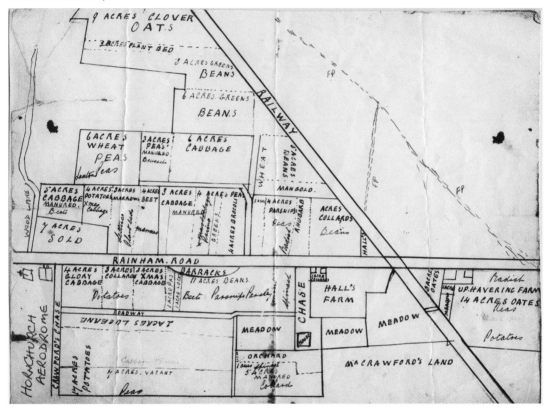

Fred Thorogood remembered his time at Elm Farm, in an interview conducted during the 1990s:

I was born in Albert Road in Romford and taken to the farm late 1915 or early 1916 when I was about two years old. Abbs Cross Lane was just a lane; it wasn't built up till about 1938 for the Hornchurch Aerodrome. Uphavering Farm and Elm Farm were all one farm at one time and joined by a small accommodation bridge over the railway line. They were capable people in those days; they had many home cures for illness. The only one I can remember is me Dad taking senna pods. Kaline poultice they used on boils and warmed camphorated oil to rub on the chest. We were all pretty healthy. I remember having measles when I was in the farmhouse, because I laid on the settee there, with all the curtains closed.

1920s farmworkers at Elm Farm, Billy Doe, Alf Hare and Ted.

PU-7800

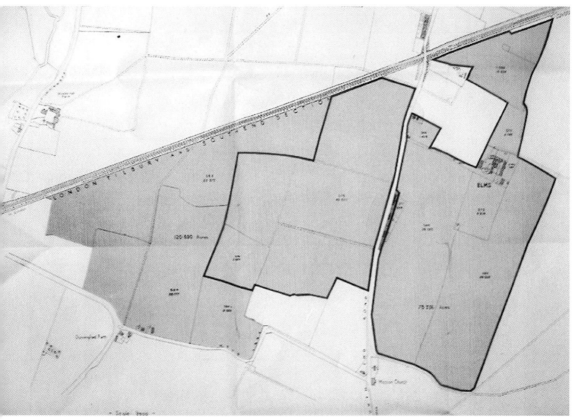

Extract from 1913 Sale Plan of Elm and Uphavering Farms

I remember Christmas at the farm more than anywhere. There was a great big fireplace in the big hall. Mum and Dad both came from big families and Mum had two brothers come up from Shoebury every Christmas. We had lots of decorations, mostly holly from our own bushes. We children would get an apple and an orange and a 'Bubbles' annual in a pillow case from Father Christmas. I don't remember the farm pond ever freezing, but I do remember it dried right up and you could walk right across it. I walked all over the pond, it was all cracks and all you could see were frogs, hundreds and hundreds of frogs.

My Grandad would get up really early to help old Bill Stokes load the cart for Spitalfields Market and because it was so early Bill would leave the farmhouse and fall asleep straight away and the horse would just go. The first place the horse would stop, without any prompting would be the 'Little Wonder Café' at Manor Park. That's about ten miles from the farm and half way to Spitalfields. It was safe enough. There'd be nothing on the roads and old Bill would wake up and have his tea. Later, of course, they got a lorry to do the work.

Ethel Page remembers working on a farm:

> I didn't like farm work much because I didn't like getting mucky. I was 12 in 1928 and I'd go tattering (potato picking) in the holidays to earn some pocket money. We'd follow Dad up the field carrying a prickle (a big basket) and pick up the potatoes and then carry them over to Clara's bench and tip them out for sorting into middlings, ware and chaps. Now wares were the large baking potatoes, middlings were the middle size potatoes and the chaps were the ones we used to take back to the farm and cook for the animals. I'd get about 10 shillings a week for that. Dad and Wally used to start work about four or five in the morning but we'd start later than that and when we got there they'd be right the length of the field.

Some other local people recall Elm Park as being famous for rhubarb, either the deep red sweet 'Daws' rhubarb or the green- stemmed 'Champagne' rhubarb suited to wine making. Many a garden in Elm Park boasts a crown of rhubarb taken from the fields around Wood Lane when they were ploughed up for development.

Ethel Page remembered growing rhubarb at Poparts Farm (Dovers Farm in South Hornchurch):

> When the rhubarb was finished the men put manure over it. Then in the spring we used to have to go and release it. That was called rhubarb puddling. You had to get a stick and open up the top of it and then go to the dungle and get some more to put on. The dungle was high up to the windows of the house and covered in a tarpaulin. It was all the manure of the farm that had been maturing the whole year. You always knew when it was ready, the smell was atrocious, and when the men took the pegs out the steam used to fly high!

Dunningford Farm c 1950

Terry Malby also remembers the rhubarb:

> I would often steal a stalk of rhubarb on my way to Dunningford School but of course I had a pouch of sugar to dip it into. If there were any sugar left I'd take another stalk on my way home again. It was delicious!

As Elm Park was built, the old farm buildings gradually disappeared and the remnants of once important manors like Wyebridge and Maylands Green, which had been owned by the Gascoynes, with them. Of the large farms and houses only the Grade II listed Bretons and Albyns Farmhouse with their associated outbuildings remain to provide a link with Elm Park's agricultural past.

Maylands Green farmhouse by the local artist Alfred Bennett Bamford in 1889. This remanant of the old Maylards Green and Wybridge manor survived into the twentieth century. After the Second World War, Hornchurch UDC built the Maylands Green Estate on the land.

Wyebridge Farm still standing as building work commenced at Elm Park, note the crane in the background.

THE BUILDING OF ELM PARK BY RICHARD COSTAIN AND SONS LTD

Albert Costain recalls in his **'Reflections'**:

> After prolonged negotiations, we purchased this land and laid out what was virtually a 'mini' new town, with houses mainly designed for clerical workers and artisans...

Between the Wars there was much concern about the health of the nation and it was acknowledged that decent housing was essential in the fight against illness and disease. People living in London and other large towns often existed in overcrowded conditions, with gas lighting, no access to a bathroom and an outdoor lavatory. Originally Liverpool based, Costain were pioneers in building large-scale housing estates in the Greater London area throughout the 1920's. Richard Rylandes Costain became managing director in 1929 and due to his foresight and enterprise the firm bought land opposite to the newly opened Fords site at Dagenham. Here Costain built the Rylandes Estate in 1931 to house Ford workers.

Whilst working at Dagenham, Costain learned that two farms in the Hornchurch area, Wyebridge and Elm Farms, were for sale. In June 1933 Costain agreed the purchase of Wyebridge Farm from the Winmill family for £53,100. The following month Costain Ltd completed the purchase of Elm Farm and Uphavering Farm from Robert Beard for a similar sum.

Richard Costain

The farms were close to the railway line that would be able to provide excellent access to London if Costain built a railway station on the new housing estate. Fortunately, Costain had learnt a valuable lesson ten years earlier in South Croydon, when the company had to provide a bus service to and from their new housing estate to the local rail station for several years. They now negotiated a deal with the railway company to build a railway station at Elm Park and have trains stop there. In order to guarantee a steady sale of properties it was essential that home owners could travel easily to their place of work.

Plans for Elm Park were announced in May 1933 and were set before Hornchurch UDC the following month. After negotiation, the Council agreed to a controversially higher density of housing than usual – 13 ½ houses per acre. The political row rumbled on, though the Council could argue that it had established additional land for road widening, a new bridge over the railway line and planting throughout the estate. Most significantly it ensured the donation of 81 acres of Wyebridge Farm, which later became part of Harrow Lodge Park. Costain had also undertaken to recruit workers via the local Labour Exchange. In January 1934 a temporary office was set up at Wyebridge Farm and work began to build Elm Park.

Building costs were comparatively cheap at this time and mortgage rates were falling. The main source of house purchase money during the 1930's, apart from local council loans or monies secured against an insurance policy, was from a building society. These were flourishing during the 30's and in April 1935 the Co-operative Permanent and Halifax Building Societies reduced their mortgage rates to four and half percent. With payments spread over 21 years a £400 house could now be purchased for 11s 8d a week. The Halifax Building Society offered 90 per cent mortgages, leaving prospective house buyers to find a down payment from £25 to £40 depending on the cost of their property. Uniquely at the time, Costain provided a variety of houses on the new Elm Park development, suited to a range of incomes. They planned to build 7,000 homes spread over 600 acres. The estate would have eight schools, five shopping areas, two churches and a cinema! This was an ambitious project indeed. In their publicity brochures they promised that:

A modest income of from £3-10s. a week can give you a freehold home in a garden setting like this at Elm Park Garden City.

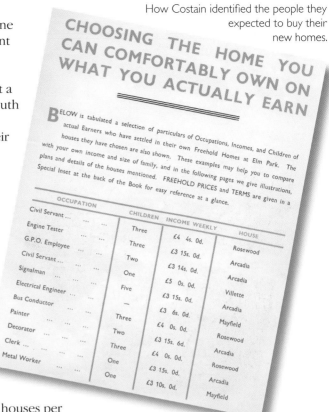

How Costain identified the people they expected to buy their new homes.

CHOOSING THE HOME YOU CAN COMFORTABLY OWN ON WHAT YOU ACTUALLY EARN

BELOW is tabulated a selection of particulars of Occupations, Incomes, and Children of actual Earners who have settled in their own Freehold Homes at Elm Park. The houses they have chosen are also shown. These examples may help you to compare with your own income and size of family, and in the following pages we give illustrations, plans and details of the houses mentioned. FREEHOLD PRICES and TERMS are given in a Special Inset at the back of the Book for easy reference at a glance.

OCCUPATION	CHILDREN	INCOME WEEKLY	HOUSE
Civil Servant ...	Three	£4 4s. 0d.	Rosewood
Engine Tester	Three	£3 15s. 0d.	Arcadia
G.P.O. Employee	Two	£3 14s. 0d.	Arcadia
Civil Servant ...	One	£5 0s. 0d.	Villette
Signalman	Five	£3 15s. 0d.	Arcadia
Electrical Engineer	—	£3 6s. 0d.	Mayfield
Bus Conductor	Three	£4 0s. 0d.	Rosewood
Painter	Two	£3 15s. 6d.	Arcadia
Decorator	Three	£4 0s. 0d.	Rosewood
Clerk ...	One	£3 15s. 0d.	Arcadia
Metal Worker	One	£3 10s. 0d.	Mayfield

George Leeder remembers:

One place that attracted me was a large sand pit situated at the junction of Elm Park Avenue and Upper Rainham Road, bordered by the railway line and Woburn Avenue. At the Rainham Road end of the pit stood a massive crane 150 feet high, the biggest I'd ever seen, reputed to have been the biggest drag-line crane in Europe. It scooped up big buckets of ballast, took it up and tipped it into the hopper at the top of the crane. Here it was crushed and fed down to the bottom of the crane which was a

Aerial photograph c. 1935
showing Wyebridge Farm where
Costain extracted sand and
gravel. Stacks of bricks can be
seen ready to build the houses
around Woodcote Avenue.

great big cement mixer. It was then taken to where it was wanted by narrow gauge railway in special hoppers which would tip it into wherever it was needed.

Brian Cornwell recalls:

There was a large gravel pit by Costain's supply yard. In winter when it froze over we children would all go skating on it.

Excavating sand at Elm Park

Elm Park cement mixer

Early residents remember the narrow two-foot gauge railway track that passed through the estate. This was built to carry supplies such as liquid mortar and concrete quickly and safely around the site and was powered by a small engine. Track was laid directly on to the ground, with junctions, turntables and sidings that could be easily picked up and re-laid where needed next.

Mini train for transporting building materials around the estate

SELLING THE HOUSES

Pioneers always get the best of everything. Those who choose early and settle at Elm Park will be able to pick sites nearer to the New Station and Main Shopping Centre.

Richard Costain's advertising brochure c1935

In his book 'Reflections' Albert Costain attributes a great deal of the success in selling houses to the imaginative ideas of one of their directors, George Warren Peachey. In successive advertising brochures Peachey wrote an introduction, directly addressing the prospective home owner. He appeals to their desire to leave **'unattractive and perhaps none too healthy surroundings'** and that with his help the way will be **'made easy for entry upon a fuller and happier life'**. Peachey then emphasises that there are no hidden costs; there are no road adoption charges, stamp duties or legal expenses. These are all included in the price. All houses are freehold with no ground rent to pay. He then speaks man to man to the bread-winner, emphasising that homes must be bought within the family's income and needs:

You must live, eat, and clothe your family as well as buy your Home, and Elm Park can provide a Plan which will enable you... to do these things while simultaneously saving money instead of paying rent. This Plan can be made between you, and me (with my wide knowledge of your difficulties...) and the World's Largest Building Society, the Halifax. It is necessary, if you are to get all the full benefits and joy out of your new home in delightful Elm Park, that you balance your budget. You must buy your home on the most comfortable terms possible.

Costain make a vivid case for home ownership

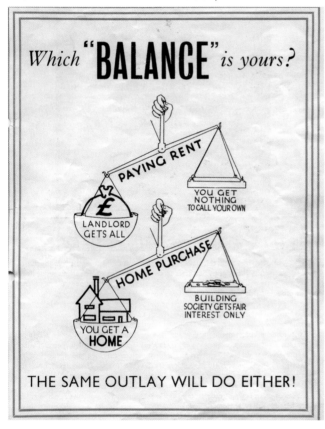

Which "BALANCE" is yours?

PAYING RENT

YOU GET NOTHING TO CALL YOUR OWN

LANDLORD GETS ALL

HOME PURCHASE

BUILDING SOCIETY GETS FAIR INTEREST ONLY

YOU GET A HOME

THE SAME OUTLAY WILL DO EITHER!

The brochure then goes on to offer a tempting choice of homes with such romantic names as Havenwood, Arcadia, Rosewood, Villette, Bramblewood or Mayfield. Compared to other building companies who merely listed their properties as Type K to Type T or Plot C this was imaginative marketing indeed. Costain were selling more than just houses, they were selling a dream. This rural romantic daydream is also reflected in the names of the first roads, which seem to indicate a countryside idyll, for example Northwood, Woodcote, Benhurst, Eyhurst, Woburn, and Park Avenues. Park Avenue was later renamed Warren Drive. It is tempting to think that Warren Peachey had something to do with the choice of this name! Gone too are the commonplace Roads or Streets, here we have Avenues, Drives, Closes, and The Broadway. The very name Elm Park was to evoke the feel of spacious parklands and aristocratic acres whilst also commemorating the Elm Farm and the elm trees that used to grow locally. This idyll could be secured for the grand sum of a pound to reserve a plot and a deposit of £25 to £30 according to your choice of house. This deposit had to be paid one week before moving in to your home.

The brochures continued to extol the virtues of the advantages of an Elm Park home. Much emphasis is placed on the abundance of garden space both front and back and to people used to cramped city streets they must have seemed spacious indeed. The promise was *that Elm Park would offer a home with a fine garden...All modern conveniences, comforts and space... everything brand new and spotless... The sunny-south of Elm Park*

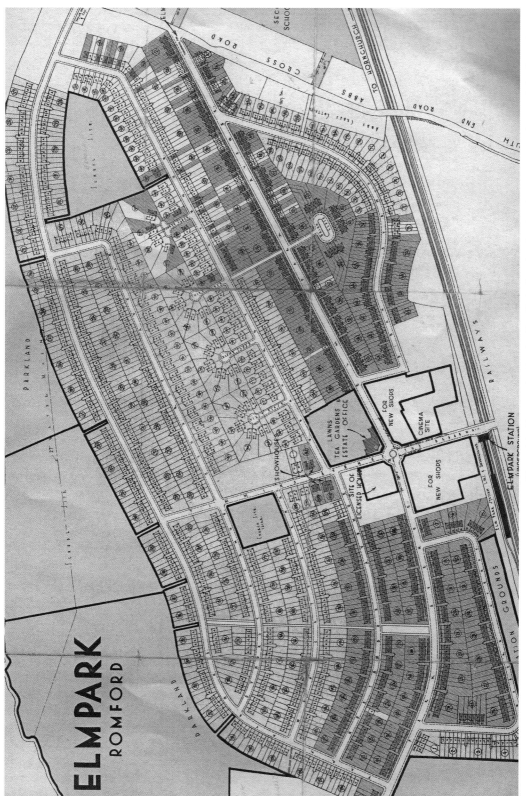

The original layout plan for the Elm Park, showing the showhomes, tea gardens and site for a cinema.

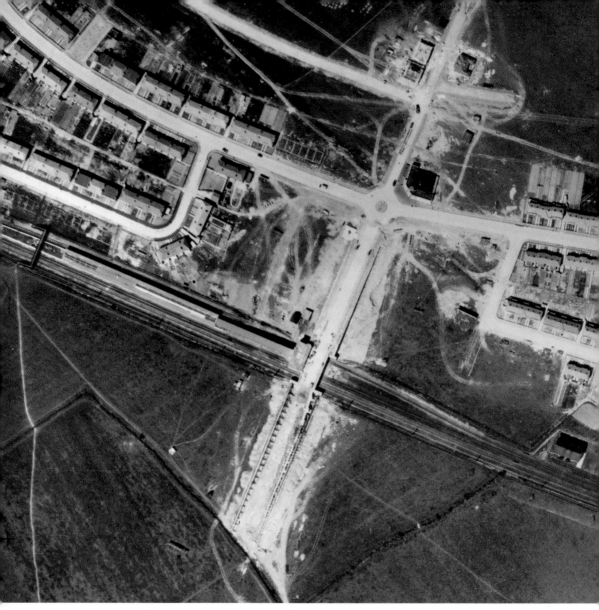

Aerial photograph from around 1935 showing Woburn Avenue and Diban Avenue, the temporary shops and railway station.

will be the Mecca of home-hunters. Who could resist such blandishments as these?

But there was resistance to house ownership. Traditionally people had rented homes and paying a mortgage seemed a huge responsibility. To encourage people to view their properties Costain laid on special buses from East Ham to Roneo Corner and then on to Elm Park. After the opening of the Elm Park station in 1935 Costain paid for free travel on the District Line from East Ham onwards for prospective clients.

Jean Hancock remembers that as a little girl in 1935 she would visit Elm Park:

A typical advert to encourage home buyers to Elm Park - Romford Recorder August 2nd 1935.

My Dad and I used to come to Elm Park for a weekly 'visit to the country'. One cold wet afternoon we came as usual and as we were passing the temporary wooden building that was the Costain estate office, a man came out and said, 'Hello Fred, I haven't seen you in years. Come in for a chat.' In no time Dad and I were inside being plied with tea and fancy cakes and being told all about the new houses and bungalows that were to be built and what a wonderful estate Elm Park would become. My father had wanted a bungalow with a big garden for a long time, so he went into all the details. We were shown plans and taken to the site in Benhurst Avenue where the first bungalows would be built. Back to the estate office, more tea and discussion before we turned out our pockets to find the pound deposit required to secure a bungalow costing £558. I remember that I contributed nine pennies (old money.) That was my savings of several weeks.

Top left: The following are all original marketing images used by Costain. Villette next to a chalet style.
Left: Chalet style house.
Top: Coronation Arcadia
Below: Costain publicity photograph of a typical garden created by early residents in the "Garden City".

Rosewood

Bungalow

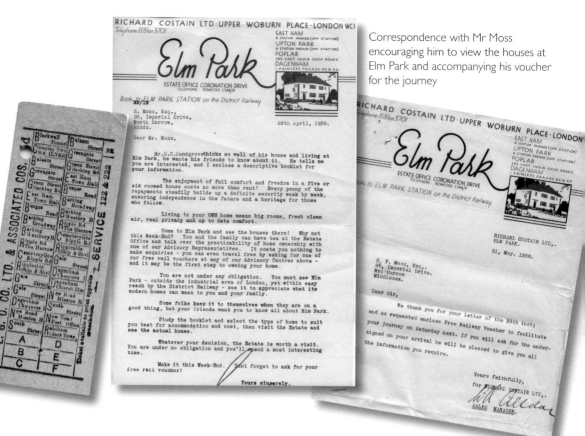

Correspondence with Mr Moss encouraging him to view the houses at Elm Park and accompanying his voucher for the journey

Prospective buyers were often treated to tea on the lawns behind the estate office and, after the release of Disney's **Snow White and the Seven Dwarfs** in 1937, a Snow White's Cottage appeared in Elm Park on the corner of Coronation Drive.

Pete Lines remembers

> When I was a little boy in the summer of 1938, I was taken as a treat to see Snow White's Cottage. I was taken in via Coronation Drive and walked up a path. It was a fair sized building made up of wood, plaster and thatch. There was a little stream in front of it with a pond at one end. A real dwarf sat there fishing. When you went in it was quite dark with several little rooms.

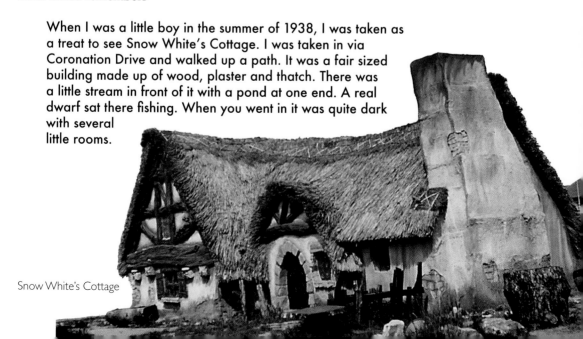

Snow White's Cottage

Snow White's Cottage

I watched the dwarves doing different things about the house. At the end of the visit I met Snow White and I talked to her! She was a young girl of about 15. It was just like meeting Father Christmas! All the time the music from the Disney film was playing. Then we came out of the cottage into Maylands Avenue. Sometimes during the summer a band played outside in the gardens. At other times recorded music played loudly from inside the house. The Hi-Ho song was especially popular. My Grandmother lived at number 58 Coronation Drive, right next door to the show house and near the cottage. My Grandmother said that the noise of the songs drove her crazy!

Later the Disney characters were replaced by wooden figures. Costain were using the popularity of the Disney film to keep children amused while their parents saw the show house and then discussed business matters.

The Costain estate office at Elm Park.

Alan Fulcher also recalls:

Richard Costain also offered free refreshments to people who looked at the properties for sale with the intent of buying one. They also had salesmen with cars, to take people around the estate. It became our weekend outing, viewing the homes. One time we even had a salesman pick us up at Elm Park station. We lived with our grandparents in Leyton at the time. What a difference from our old home to the new house in Fernbank Avenue, like paradise to us children, so many fields to play in.

One of the Costain brochures features a photograph entitled 'Floodlit houses at Elm Park'. This surely indicates that, at least some of the time, the estate was lit up at night to encourage evening visits from busy day workers. A lot of information was communicated to residents via the **Elm Park Pictorial** the first estate newspaper ever published by Richard Costain Ltd. This enterprising company would try anything to promote their houses.

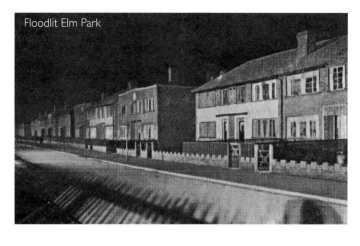
Floodlit Elm Park

The most important selling feature of any new housing estate was the show house. Costain's publicity photographs reveal smartly furnished show homes complete with curtains, beds, dining table and chairs and a kitchen fitted out with a butler style sink. The kitchen seems the strangest to modern eyes for where are the appliances that we rely on today? But the brochure promises that in '*their woman designed Arcadia kitchen, this scientific headquarters of housekeeping …is the most practical… fitted storage cabinets supplement a large larder…a deep porcelain sink with chromium taps (hot and cold) is pleasantly placed under the side window. Beneath its draining board is a modern gas copper for easy boiling on wash days…a domestic boiler is neatly installed beside a commodious brush cupboard and the position of the gas cooker is arranged by the back door so that cooking fumes may escape readily*'.

The other house designs are equally highly recommended and lavishly praised.

Elm Park Pictorial – heralded as the first ever housing estate newspaper

THE FIRST ESTATE NEWSPAPER EVER PUBLISHED

ELM PARK PICTORIAL

the New HOME *CENTRE*

" TO SHOW THE FACTS " "TO TELL THE TRUTHS "

Published by Richard Costain Ltd *House Builders for 65 Years*

OLD ENGLAND'S BROAD ACRES FOR HER BEST HOMELAND

Arcadia lounge looking towards the French windows and the loggia 1937

Arcadia lounge towards bay window 1937

Hallway of a Coronation Arcadia 1937

Arcadia kitchen 1937

Showhome bathroom 1937

Arcadia bedroom 1937

Another showhouse bedroom 1937

Box room 1937

Elm Park Assembly Hall photographed in 1937, before the annexe was built

Another significant factor in selling homes to prospective buyers was the promise of a local social life. In the days before most people owned a car or a television, being able to find entertainment on your own doorstep was very important. Costain built the Assembly Hall and presented it to the Residents' Association for the continued benefit of the Elm Park community. By 1937 the Assembly Hall features in Costain pamphlets, showing a festive hall packed with families. Billed as a 'Recreation Hall and Theatre', the Assembly Hall's position as the hub of the Elm Park community was crucial.

Dance at the Assembly Hall

OPENING THE ESTATE MAY 1935

The Elm Park estate was officially opened on Saturday 18th May 1935 by Sir Edward Hilton Young, Minister of Health. He was accompanied by his wife, Kathleen, who was the widow of Captain Robert Scott, the famous Antarctic explorer. The Minister arrived at Elm Park station at 2.45pm. A decorated saddle tank engine pulled into Elm Park Station, pulling three coaches. The front of the engine bore the legend **The Elm Park Special**. After assembling on the platform the guests of honour walked past a line of about a dozen Elm Park children. The girls were dressed in pretty frilly frocks and crisp white ankle socks, whilst the boys wore blazers and short trousers. All the children stood politely to attention with their hands behind their backs. In Woburn Avenue excitement was intense as onlookers crowded along the tracks to watch the spectacle. A large marquee stood by the track, doubtless to entertain the dignitaries later on.

Then, with great ceremony the party was conducted up the ramp from the platform by the stationmaster. The ramp was decorated with colourful flags and bunting. There was no central barrier to hamper the progress of the party as people surged up the incline. At the top of the slope the metal barriers were closed and Sir Edward was invited to open the gates with a silver key. As he had lost an arm whilst commanding a gun turret on the **Vindictive** during the blockade of Zeebrugge in 1918 (for which he had been awarded a bar to his DSC for his bravery) the key was removed from its case and handed to him in order to perform the ceremony.

Dagenham Girl Pipers who performed at the opening ceremony in 1935

Once through the gates the party erupted out on to the road. There were no shops on the approach to the station but poles had been erected along the roadside and hung with festive streamers. The Dagenham Girl Pipers led the way down The Broadway to Elm Park Avenue. As they reached the bottom of the hill they led off to each side to allow Sir Edward to come forward and pass through an ornamental arch which proclaimed 'Welcome to Elm Park'. A blizzard of coloured paper poured from the top of it as the party went under the archway. Sir Edward then cut a tape and climbed on to a specially built platform. Loudspeakers broadcast the speeches to the huge waiting crowds. There was much praise expressed for everyone associated with the project. The Co-operation between all the agencies involved was applauded; Sir Edward then spoke of his pleasure at seeing **"so many happy and cheerful faces… and everyone's pleasure at the re-housing of so many families on such a beautiful and healthy site under the best modern conditions…in comparison to the old homes… in the slums"**.

The "Welcome To Elm Park" arch which greeted Hilton Young in 1935 remained for some years afterwards.

Many other local dignitaries attended the ceremony, including the Mayors of West and East Ham, members of the Hornchurch and Romford Urban District Councils and the local Romford and Stratford MPs. They saw Margaret Cutbush receive a silver cup for making the most improvement in her education since coming to Elm Park and baby Rena Jeffrey of Diban Avenue receiving gifts for being born in Elm Park closest to Jubilee Day. (King George V and Queen Mary had celebrated their Silver Jubilee on May 6th.) As he was unable to be present, Peter Day of Elm Park Avenue was to have his prize forwarded to him. Later the crowds were able to enjoy displays from the Dagenham Girl Pipers and the Legion of Frontiersmen band, and see some trick equestrian riding. There were cookery and other demonstrations and afternoon tea was served!

The Romford Times claimed that the estate had been built at a cost of about £3.5 million and became the largest single private housing estate in England. Eventually it was expected to house 35,000 people. Pride was expressed in the sourcing of so many building materials locally, including the bricks and windows.

EARLY YEARS IN ELM PARK
1934-1939

George Leeder remembers:

> We had to sell our piano to pay for the deposit on our new house.

W hat was life really like for the new home owners in those early days? According to the publicity brochures life would be like a little bit of heaven once you had moved to Elm Park but was the reality slightly different?

Early residents would have had a struggle to get to work before the new station was opened in May 1935 and even bus services were limited. There was no direct bus route to Romford until 1939 when the Upper Rainham Road was finally made up. In January 1939 the Romford Times reported that the roundabout at the junction of Elm Park Avenue and Timmins Avenue (now St. Nicholas Avenue) was hazardous with several minor accidents occurring there. This area also suffered from poor street lighting and many local roads had no lighting at all. There was a lack of telephone kiosks; a serious situation in the days when home telephones were rare. But, these things were of no concern to children who revelled in the freedom of the countryside around Elm Park.

Sheila Fry remembers:

> I was ten when we came to Elm Park in 1934. One of my favourite pastimes was wandering over the railway hill down towards Suttons Lane. It was all fields over there, divided by clear streams and ditches. On a Sunday I would pick watercress from the streams and we'd have it for Sunday tea with winkles or shrimps and celery. But my all-time favourite was watercress and Marmite sandwiches!

Ena Risby was four years old when she moved to Elm Park in 1938 and recalls:

> Our back garden overlooked open fields and the bottom end of Maybank Avenue was nothing but fields. I remember how countrified the area was. South End Road ran the other end of Maybank with ditches and hedgerows running either side of the road in front of the houses...and Wood Lane again with ditches and hedgerows going into fields on either side. My parents and neighbours would walk across the fields from the back of our house to the White Hart public house in Hacton Lane, Upminster. There was a small open space where a ditch ran through, which continued along the bottom of the back gardens in Morecambe

Close where we would run down, jump the clear, sparkling water, and up the other side (so exhilarating) on our way to the sweet shop near the corner of Wood Lane. Opposite the shop were two very old cottages and next to them a small church. I remember it being deserted and we played in there. A lot of dusty prayer books had been left inside.

When new residents moved in there was great competition for their custom from local tradesmen. Free gifts of a welcome hamper, or a china tea set, or apostle spoons were on offer and the milkmen were especially anxious to secure new customers.

Elm Park Library exhibition comments book 1995

United Dairies left a complimentary box with milk, eggs, and butter on the day we moved in.

George Leeder remembers:

We would have weekend trips to Elm Park to watch the house being built. The big day arrived in August, a lorry arrived and was loaded. We waved goodbye to our neighbours in West Ham and we were off. We soon arrived at the Estate Office sited on the junction of Elm Park Avenue and Timmins Avenue by the roundabout. We collected our key and made our way through the stacks of bricks and timber to our house, plot 141c Northwood

A plate given to early residents by one of the dairies

Avenue. The furniture was unloaded and we began to settle in. The first priority was to stock the larder! Milk was no problem for when we arrived at the house, there was a milkman, waiting on the step with a pint of milk in his hand.
'Have our milk and we will give you a free tea service,' he said. He was from Hitchman's Dairies and that was the first job completed. We then went off to the shops. Costain had built a row of temporary shops each side of the estate office. There was Sam Weller who sold radios and bicycles and piano acccordions...Hollicks...they sold newspapers, and ran a post office and a library. The opposite corner was taken up by the Gray's Co-op. On the whole there was a fine selection of goods.

WHERE EVERYTHING IS NEW, CLEAN, HEALTHY & COMPLETE

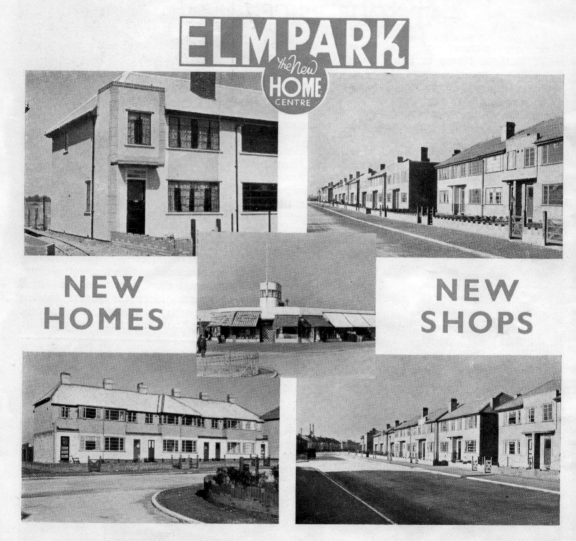

ELM PARK
The New
HOME CENTRE

NEW HOMES

NEW SHOPS

NEW ROADS FREE FROM COSTS

Above are some snapshots of Elm Park, showing the wide, sunny avenues and ample front gardens. No overcrowding here, and no old property to spoil the outlook or to let down the tone of the district. A new community in a new world, of which every home owner is proud and contented.

NEW SCHOOLS, PARKS, CINEMAS, HOTELS
in course of erection.

This page from the first sales brochure for the estate includes three views of Elm Park Avenue, Woburn Avenue as well as the temporary shops and viewing tower.

It is interesting to note that one of the first shops on the new estate included a bicycle shop that also provided radios and piano accordions. The bicycle would have been the main method of transport for many, while the radio was the main source of entertainment.

The Mayfield

The Villette

The Bramblewood. Was this design ever used in Elm Park?

The Coronation Arcadia

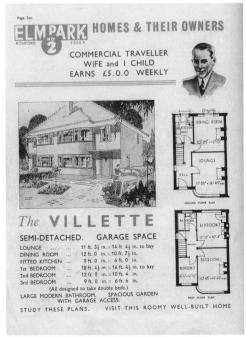

Plenty of room for all family needs

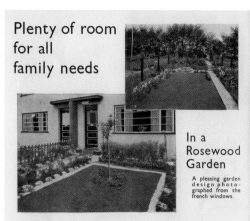

In a Rosewood Garden

A pleasing garden design photographed from the french windows.

The "ROSEWOOD" GARDEN TERRACE HOME

The "Rosewood" type of home is one of the most spacious and practical houses at Elm Park and as such has been one of popular choice since the early days of the Garden City.

The end type permits the building of a garage, if required. Those in the centre offer some economy in heating, by reason of the absence of the third outer wall, while it is also a little more economical in the weekly cost.

Both middle and end houses are identical in number and size of rooms, and all fittings and finishes are of equal quality. This seven-roomed home is planned throughout on practical lines, affording two living rooms and fitted kitchen (with a large hall) on the ground floor, and three double bedrooms and fitted bathroom upstairs.

The kitchen is particularly well-planned, with fitted dresser for dry goods and brushes, and a folding cook's table ; large storage cupboard under the staircase ; porcelain sink with chromium hot and cold taps, draining board, and gas copper for wash-day boiling.

An economical hot water system is provided for bathroom and kitchen, heated from the dining room fire. The linen cupboard upstairs is also heated from the same source.

Handsome fireplaces and a wide choice of beautiful decorations give the "Rosewood" home an appearance to be proud of. It is a home in which it is a joy to live and show your friends. Ample garden space gives you every opportunity to provide for your table and your floral decorations at practically no cost.

FOR INCOMES OF £4 WEEKLY UP

THE "ROSEWOOD" HOME

1st BEDROOM	-	13 ft. 0 in. × 10 ft. 4 in.
2nd BEDROOM	-	12 ft. 0 in. × 10 ft. 4 in.
3rd BEDROOM	-	10 ft. 11 in. × 6 ft. 6 in.

(All take double beds comfortably.)

DINING ROOM	-	12 ft. 0 in. × 10 ft. 7½ in.
DRAWING ROOM	-	13 ft. 0 in. × 11 ft. 3½ in.
FITTED KITCHEN	-	8 ft. 7 in. × 6 ft. 0 in.

Large Hall. Fitted Bathroom.

COMPARE THESE PLANS WITH THE DESCRIPTION OF THE "ROSEWOOD" HOME ON THE PRECEDING PAGE.

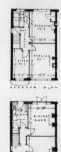

INCLUSIVE FREEHOLD PRICE
and
SIMPLE PURCHASE TERMS

(See inset at the back of this book.)

The Rosewood

The Havenwood

The Hawthorne

Seven Large Rooms

Two Large Gardens

The "HAVENWOOD" GARDEN TERRACE HOMES

(With End Types Available)

The "Havenwood" home has been designed to give the greatest possible family accommodation to the modest wage-earner—accommodation which is unrivalled in any other housing centre. A study of the plans on the next page will show how this is achieved. The "Havenwood" homes, built in short terraces, are set well back in spacious garden plots. The terraces are sufficiently short to lend a pleasing frontal appearance to the houses. The space that is gained by the use of this alternative to building in semi-detached pairs is actually incorporated in the houses, as will readily be seen from an examination of the plans and measurements. Accordingly a really sizeable home is placed easily within the reach of an income of from £3 10s. a week, and nothing is lacking in the fittings and equipment which are standard for Elm Park homes.

A feature of the "Havenwood Home" is the introduction of "coupled" rooms downstairs. This gives the owner choice of furnishing two separate living-rooms, divided by a pair of wide doors, or of economically treating the double area as one room and furnishing accordingly, with one floor covering and combined furniture. The latter is an excellent modern way of making the most of space, at least cost, both for living and entertaining.

Three double bedrooms, with fitted modern bathroom adjoining, provide ample convenience for a family, while the labour-saving kitchen is fitted with cabinet storage, gas copper, porcelain sink, draining board and chromium taps (hot and cold).

End houses of the "Havenwood" type have space for garage, and the advantage of a semi-detached house. As there are a limited number only of end houses, inspection and booking should be made early.

Garden space both back and front is on a generous scale and all gates, fences and front pathways are completed.

The HAWTHORNE HOME

Terrace Type ACCOMMODATION

The popular SIX-ROOMED home at Elm Park. This is the most completely equipped and really commodious house ever offered at anything near its price. Thousands of people pay more in rent for two-roomed flats than the Hawthorne home costs to BUY.

FIRST BEDROOM : 10' 7½" × 10' 7".
SECOND BEDROOM : 8' 9" × 7' 0".
THIRD BEDROOM : 9' 9" × 6' 4".
(All take double beds if required.)
LIVING ROOM : 13' 6" × 13' 2½".
FITTED KITCHEN : 10' 7" × 9' 3".
LARGE FITTED BATHROOM.

The double-bed space afforded in each of the three bedrooms is a feature obtained by placing the bathroom at the foot of the staircase. The bath is of white porcelain enamel, fitted with chromium taps, and with a square-panelled side. Constant hot water is available, heated from the Living Room fire, which also heats the oven, hot-plate and linen cupboard. Free Gas Copper is installed in the Kitchen, which is fitted with complete cabinet accommodation, folding table, sink and drainer-board, etc. Furnished HAWTHORNE Home at Elm Park reveals the undoubted charm and convenience of its design. See Plans below.

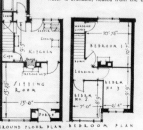

GROUND FLOOR PLAN   BEDROOM PLAN

INCLUSIVE FREEHOLD PRICE

AND SIMPLE PURCHASE TERMS
See Inset at back

George Leeder continues:

Building was going on at a fast pace and Woodcote and Eyhurst Avenues were well on the way. Costain was building the Assembly Hall and on bank holidays they always laid on entertainment of some sort: fairs, competitions, dance socials and various other things. A Residents' Association was started up and also a gardening club. The social life of the estate was beginning to burst into life. When the Assembly Hall was completed Costain brought in a celebrity to perform the opening ceremony. This was done in style. There was a piece of railway line along side the railway fence in Woburn Avenue, this line was extended along Elm Park Avenue to where The Elm Park pub now stands and a railway engine and carriage brought the celebrity to the estate office. From there they walked down to the Assembly Hall for the opening ceremony. I believe the celebrity was Evelyn Laye the well known stage actress.

Evelyn Holloway recalls:

We moved to Elm Park in March 1939 when I was five years old. I remember going to the Estate Office and choosing wallpaper and paint for the house. All the houses had electricity and we had a gas copper for washing clothes. Not all the houses were built or the roads made up and I remember fields all around.

Ken Elliott remembers a special occasion:

When I was about ten or eleven, which would be about 1938, I heard that Jean Batten the famous aviator was coming to Elm Park. I jumped on my bike and cycled from my home in Dagenham down country lanes to Elm Park Station. There she was, standing surrounded by a crowd of spectators. She looked like a film star, with her dark hair and glamorous poise. Jean Batten was called the Garbo of the skies and now I could see why.

Jean Batten (1909-1982) was born in New Zealand. Inspired by Charles Lindberg's Trans Atlantic flight in 1927, she learnt to fly, always encouraged by her mother to compete in a man's world. In 1934 she was feted in Australia and New Zealand when she broke her rival Amy Johnson's world record of a solo flight from England to Australia. She beat Amy's record by four days. Amy Johnson (1903 -1941) also visited Elm Park. Residents remember her standing in an open topped car wearing a white flying suit. Amy died in 1941 whilst working for the Air Transport Auxiliary. She became lost in fog and low cloud over the River Thames. Forced to bale out her body was never discovered.

Halifax Building Society paying book

ILFORD BRANCH.
47, Cranbrook Road.
Office Hours: 9-30 to 4. Saturday: 9 to 12.
Friday Evenings, 6 to 8 p.m.
All enquiries and remittances to be sent to above address.

ELM PARK

Roll No. A 427975

IN ACCOUNT WITH THE

HALIFAX
BUILDING SOCIETY

In all communications please quote above Roll No

RICHARD COSTAIN LIMITED.
A 1998
18 UPPER WOBURN PLACE,
LONDON, W.C.1
Telephone EUSTON 5701.
LONDON June 25th 1938
RECEIVED of H. F. Moss Esq.
the Sum of Twenty-one pounds
Completion of Deposit on House
843B. Elms Farm Rd Elm Park
£21 : 0 : 0
FOR & ON BEHALF OF
RICHARD COSTAIN LTD.
A. J. King
ESTATE MANAGER

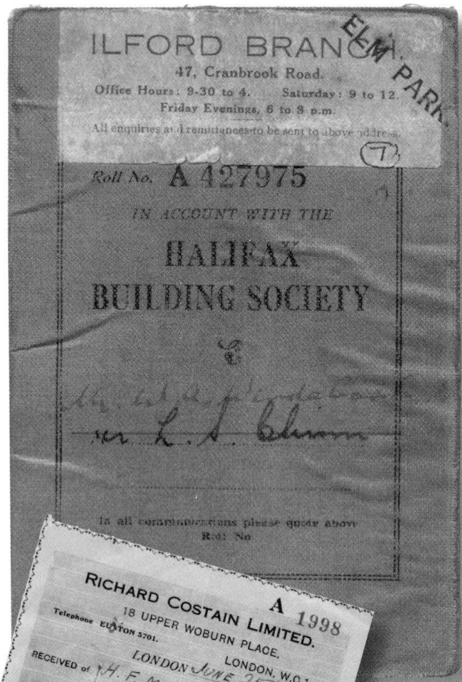

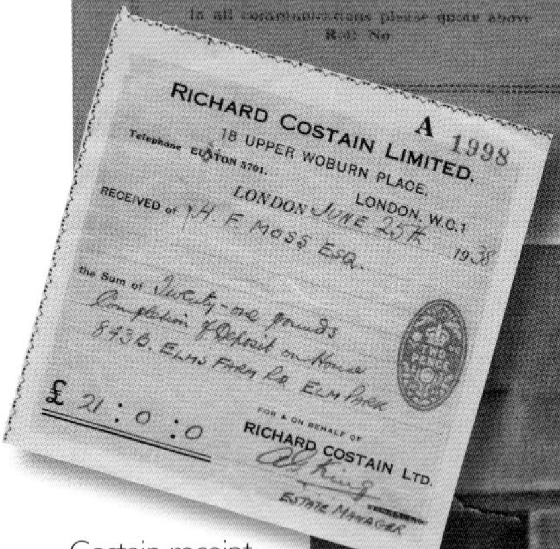

Costain receipt for completion of deposit payment

Jean Hancock recalls:

We finally moved to Elm Park in 1936. At that time I only remember Costain's office, a sweet shop cum post office, a butchers shop, and I think a little general store situated on a very rough field. There was no pavement and no made up road. Benhurst Avenue was still not completed and the Closes had not been named. The bungalows had temporary plot numbers. The foundations were laid in Eyhurst Avenue and we watched the houses being built. In the hot summer holidays we walked all over the fields, which stretched from Eyhurst to the Hornchurch Road. In a year or two all the houses, bungalows, and shops were going up The Broadway (up the hill to the station) and Broadway Parade. There was no building at all for

James Hills outside his new home in Elm Park Avenue

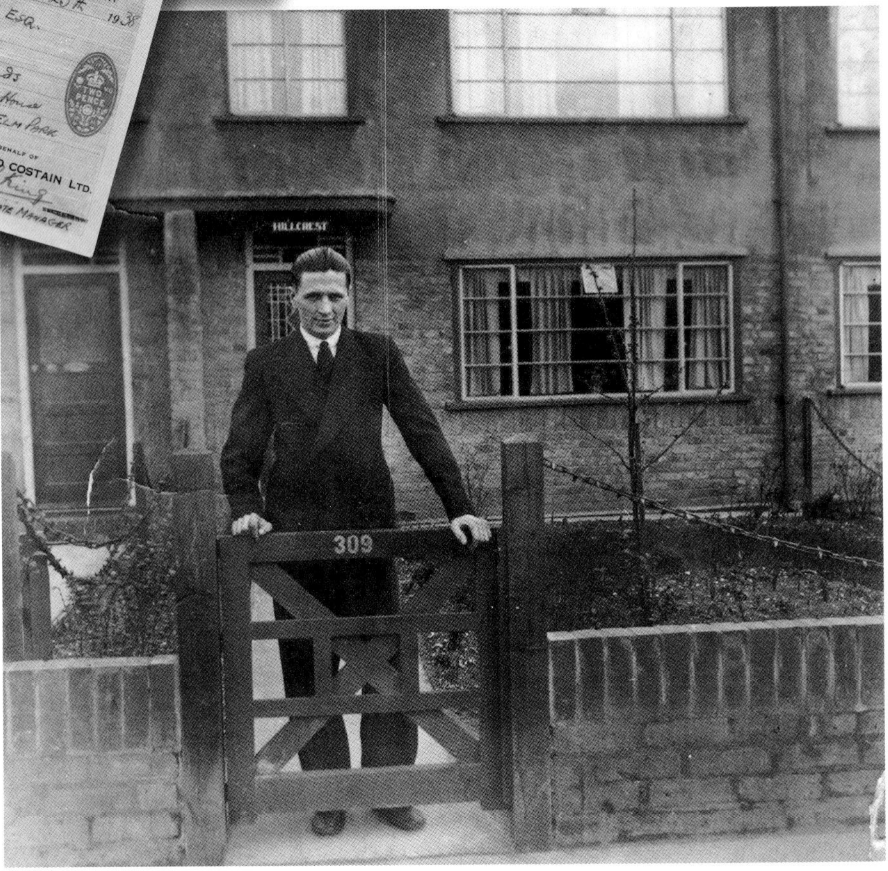

two or three years on the south side of Elm Park station and we used to take picnics over there. We'd cross the stream at the foot of the hill and walk for miles, past the old farm buildings, and around Hornchurch Aerodrome buildings and the airfield.

George Leeder recalls an unusual handout as building started south of the railway line in 1938:

A big farmhouse stood by the side of the railway line, by the bridge, on the South End Road. The old house was surrounded by a big orchard of fruit trees, apples, pears, cherries and other fruits. When the buildings were pulled down, the trees were handed over to the Residents Association, so they could allocate trees to the people who wanted them. Everyone was given one half of a raffle ticket and on the Sunday everyone went to the orchard and located the tree with their number on it. They dug it out and took it home. It was a strange sight to see people all over the estate struggling along with large trees on top of vans, barrows and even the local coalman with his horse and cart!

Rose Cordell and Jeffrey Hills, Elm Park Avenue

PAMELA COVENTRY

Tragically the peaceful life of the new estate was shattered on January 18th 1939 when nine-year-old Pamela Coventry failed to return home from the afternoon session at Benhurst Primary School. The story has been covered elsewhere (see bibliography for details) but briefly the facts are as follows. Having had her dinner, Pamela left her home in Morecambe Close to walk to back to school for the afternoon. School friends waited for her on the corner of Benhurst Avenue but she failed to arrive. The alarm was raised by her stepmother when she didn't come home after school ended. Local police searched for Pamela until midnight and the next day her naked body was found in a ditch, under a hedge, in Wood Lane by a night watchman.

Sir Bernard Spilsbury, the eminent forensic pathologist, conducted the post mortem. He said that her last meal had been eaten about 12.45pm and death had occurred about an hour after. She had been strangled following a blow to the chin and sexually assaulted. On her chest was found the stub of a home-made cigarette. She had been tied with wire commonly used for wireless aerials, black copper cable with tarred string attached, as if it had been used in gardening to string up vegetables.

Men from RAF Hornchurch were drafted in to help hunt for clues, namely her missing clothes. The police searched the derelict Wybridge Farm and its outbuildings, as well as local fields and allotments. Later, details of her clothes were released to the public in order to increase the likelihood of finding them. People were urged to search outhouses and garages and look for wire similar to that found on her body. And police instigated house-to-house enquiries. On February 2nd 1939 Leonard Richardson (28) of Coronation Drive, who worked for a Dagenham firm manufacturing chemicals was arrested and charged with Pamela's murder. Pamela's Wellington boots had been found in Abbs Cross Lane and a school badge, three buttons and some black cable was found wrapped in newspaper near Elm Park Station. The evidence against Richardson was all circumstantial and at his trial at the Old Bailey the jury quickly passed a note to the judge and he was acquitted due to lack of evidence. The foreman of the jury shook his hand as he left the court. The police never charged anyone else for Pamela's murder.

ELM PARK SOCIAL LIFE

In a canteen, in the centre of a field, the Elm Park Residents' Association held their inaugural meeting as reported in the Romford Times of 24th July 1935.

The committee of the Elm Park Residents Association photographed outside the Assembly Hall

Elm Park Residents leaflet

FRIENDSHIP

"Life has no pleasure nobler than that of friendship."—Johnson

That pleasant human intercourse called friendship which does so much to smooth the path of life is always to be found where there is a community of interest.

In home-ownership, in the embarkation on a new and fuller life amid pleasant and stimulating surroundings such as prevail at Elm Park, there is to be found, by all who desire it, that common interest which is the key to friendship.

Four years ago people who came to live at Elm Park founded a Residents' Association for the purpose of establishing contact and deriving from this community of interest both friendship and tangible mutual benefit.

To-day the Elm Park Residents' Association, democratically controlled, and staffed by voluntary workers, is the largest organisation of home-owners in Essex.

Through its experience of public affairs it serves the residents in a most practical way by getting things done.

By its development of social, residential and sporting facilities, it has given a new and wider meaning to life to many of its members and their families.

Above all, it stands as the symbol of friendship, extending the glad hand of welcome to each and every newcomer.

WILL YOU JOIN US?

J. J. P. BRIDGEN,
Chairman,
Elm Park Residents' Association.

(A postcard to the Secretary, The Assembly Hall, Elm Park, will bring you full information about the Association).

According to the Romford Times the temporary committee of the Residents' Association expressed gratification at the large numbers attending this inaugural meeting, which included many ladies. The women would be particularly interested in issues that affected them, namely the shopping facilities and transport to and from Romford. Mr Pearce (later to be elected Chairman of the group) stated that the association would be non-political and only concern itself with local affairs. Mr Pearce predicted that many of the audience would stay in Elm Park for the rest of their lives and so would want to be as happy and comfortable as possible. The rules of the Association were approved and subscription fees set at one shilling per year. Richard Costain Ltd sent a cheque for five guineas and a letter of congratulations on the formation of the association. This met with applause and approval and it was agreed to send a letter of thanks to the building firm.

By the 14th August 1935 the Romford Times was reporting that two associations had been formed in Elm Park, a Residents' Association and a Sports and Social Club. The tennis section had its own grass courts and a tournament was currently in progress and a football team had been entered for the Brentwood Charity Cup competition. The first leg would be a home match against the Gas Light and Coke Company! Children's sports activities had also been arranged. Mr A. P. Costain had agreed to be president. By January 1939 Mr Bridgen, Chairman of the Residents' Association, was calling for funds to build a much needed extension to the Assembly Hall in order to make more provision for the youngsters of Elm Park.

Tennis courts in the late forties, a converted Anderson shelter provided changing facilities.

The proposed cinema in Elm Park failed to materialize. However, on 3rd August 1935, the Towers Cinema opened in Hornchurch with an enormous number of people flocking to the first night and hundreds more being turned away. The opening ceremony was performed by Councillor Davis, leader of Hornchurch Urban District Council.

The entertainment that followed consisted of two feature films, a newsreel, followed by a live stage performance from Paul Lukas and his orchestra with the St. David Singers. The evening ended with a reception and dance in the opulent café and ballroom.

The Towers Cinema

A feature of the cinema's façade was the red and green neon lighting that set the frontage ablaze with light. The interior was luxuriously furnished and could seat 2,000 people. On the balcony were six boxes, each equipped with hearing apparatus. The technical equipment was most up to date and maintained by 30 staff, under the manager, Mr Sewell who had transferred from the Capitol Cinema, Upminster. A film was taken of the crowds entering at the opening ceremony which was shown on the programme the following week.

Al Fulcher remembers:

> Our entertainment was going to the cinema at least once a week and of course the Saturday matinee for children. The episodes would continue each Saturday morning – Flash Gordon is just one film that I remember. We would go to the Towers Cinema by catching a number 66 bus from Hornchurch station or the single-decker that ran up Abbs Cross Lane.

Elm Park Library exhibition comments book 1995

We went to Brownies, Cubs, Scouts, and Guides. We danced at the Elm Park Hotel and the Assembly Hall. We joined the drama group run by Mrs Flack, who was also Guide leader and we were in various pantomimes and dramas. We went to the Towers for the pictures and Romford for the Ritz, Havana, Plaza and occasionally the old Laurie Cinema in the Market Place. When we first moved to Elm Park we used to go to the children's pictures in the Assembly Hall, to see Charlie Chaplin.

Sheila Fry remembers:

During the early War years I was training to be a dance teacher and once I got my certificate I started my own dance school, the Northwood School of Dance based at the Assembly Hall. When I started I had just one pupil, but by the end of the first year I had 100! In 1941 I put on a charity pantomime at May and Bakers with my dance troupe the 'Spitfire Babes.' Children from my dance school performed in shows and films such as 'Chitty Chitty Bang Bang' and 'The Prime of Miss Jean Brodie'. In 1971 a group of my girls performed on television in the talent show 'Opportunity Knocks' with presenter Hughie Green.

Del Ramsey remembers:

Sometimes we'd go over to the Airfield site, although this was strictly patrolled. The dugouts would be filled with water and this attracted lots of wildlife such as frogs, toads and even snakes. Another way to find frogs and toads was to stand by a road drain, especially after it had rained. There were loads. Even today, I admit to looking down at the road drains after a rain shower to see if I can see any frogs – old habits die hard!

CIVIC WEEK IN ELM PARK

'All sections of community life on the estate are participating in the eight days festivities', reported the Romford Times of 12th April 1939.

During April 1939 the Romford Times covered the exciting gala week which was staged on the new Elm Park Garden City estate. Supported by Costain as a marketing exercise, Easter Week 8th to 15th April was earmarked as the promotional event of the year for Elm Park. Everything was free and refreshments were provided at most activities.

The Broadway and Assembly Hall were decorated with colourful bunting and flags, and the Assembly Hall was floodlit at night. Inside the hall trophies were on display and the walls covered with paintings and drawings by local children. Elm Park had taken on the **'appearance of a popular holiday resort where but a few years ago the stretch of land between Abbs Cross Lane and Rainham Road on which Elm Park is built was open fields.'**

Highlights of the festival included a shop window display competition, where people were invited to guess the winners of the event in the correct order!

Half page advert from the Romford Times of 5th April 1939 promoting Elm Park Civic Week

Local shopkeepers were expected to learn a great deal about shopping psychology from listening to customers' comments. The winning shops were J Hollick, Meyers Stores and the Grays Co-operative Society. Elm Park traders were also able to showcase their wares at the Assembly Hall setting out their stalls to advertise their business. A mannequin parade using professional models allowed women to see the latest fashions and facilities were available for ordering goods.

Pretty brunette Miss Alice Martin, aged 17, had been voted 'Miss Elm Park,' chosen from dozens of contestants at a ball held at the Assembly Hall. She had lived in Diban Avenue for three years and although she worked in a shoe shop her ambition was to become a singer. A waltz competition was won by Mrs Wilson of Woburn Avenue and Mr Marsden of 54th Squadron RAF Hornchurch. Cunningly, Costain included a competition that was only open to non-residents. The five show houses in Coronation Drive and Maybank Avenue each had one item incorrectly fitted – for example a soap dish placed upside down. Competitors had to thoroughly check the houses and list the deliberate mistakes in order of inconvenience. The winners came from as far afield as West Kensington and Acton.

The event became a victim of its own success when dozens of disappointed children had to be turned away as the Assembly Hall was full for the Saturday morning picture show, which lasted two and a half hours. The show included silent films, talkies, dramas, cartoons, and instructive films! In the afternoon there was a programme for adults who were treated to George Formby's hit 'No Limit' amongst other films.

Other activities included a carnival fete with a decorated pram competition. The winner was toddler Pamela Christopher, with her doll's pram covered in spring flowers, but overwhelmed by all the attention, she burst into tears and refused to go up and collect her prize. Several other children started crying in sympathy!

Easter Monday ended with a magnificent firework display and an all star concert cabaret at the Assembly Hall. Davy Burnaby and Michael North, stars of radio, stage and screen were the hosts for the evening. They introduced the audience to a brand new dance with actions (like the Lambeth Walk) which they had created. Having watched the steps demonstrated with a willing volunteer, the audience were soon dancing the new steps and actions. Parry Jones, the B.B.C. and Covent Garden tenor, sang three songs and Cyril Shields the illusionist baffled the audience with his magic. Harry Leader's band entertained throughout the evening. A talent competition completed the second half of the evening which was won by Mrs Jones of South End Road impersonating Marie Lloyd.

Cookery demonstrations were given in the Assembly Hall and a cake making competition held. Displays were given by the Men's Gymnasium and Physical Culture Club at a midweek dance at the Assembly Hall. The Elm Park Men's Club had an open house evening where people could wander into the Assembly Hall and taste the delights of table tennis, darts, snooker, billiards, and fun competitions. Later in the week a whist drive was held there.

Elm Park Men's Club

Elm Park came to a standstill on Thursday due to a traffic jam of prams and pushchairs as Mums struggled to get into the Assembly Hall for the judging of the baby show. There were so many entrants that judging took four hours and no one envied the judges, Dr Vallance and Miss Casting, their difficult choice. Special prizes went to Mrs Hill whose baby was born in Civic Week and to Mrs Lane for having twin boys.

For sports enthusiasts there was an open tennis tournament where, except in the finals, matches were played in single sets. For football fans there were two exciting matches. The first saw the Elm Park A team defeat Holy Cross 3-2 at the Roneo ground in the Hornchurch Charity Cup Final. Then, crowds of several thousands watched the final of the Ilford Hospital Charity Cup, between Ilford Electric and Elm Park. The local crowd had the satisfaction of seeing their team defeat their opponents 2-1.

The finale of Civic Week was a fancy dress ball attended by as many as could squeeze into the Assembly Hall. Balloons and streamers ensured a party mood and prizes were awarded for the week's competitions.

It is interesting to note how the many prize winners listed in the newspaper have their full address given. Where they lived was most important and possibly one of the main points of the exercise. The focus was after all on putting Elm Park on the map.

CLUBS AND SOCIETIES

ELM PARK HORTICULTURAL GUILD

Jeremy Wilkes, General and Trading Secretary, writes an account of the history of Elm Park Horticultural Guild:

To encourage potential buyers and to make the new Elm Park estate look attractive, Costain the builders and developers sponsored a 'Best Front Garden Competition.' A committee was formed of local residents to administer and judge the event, and out of this the Elm Park Gardens Guild was created. In an effort to support a communal spirit flower shows were organised and trophies donated by, amongst others, the Halifax Building Society, Messrs. Taylor Walker and the Elm Park Residents Association.

The first show took place on 24th April 1937. There were 15 classes in which members staged 47 exhibits. Summer and autumn shows followed, held in school halls (Benhurst and Ayloff)

Elm Park Townswomen's Guild was formed in 1937. This photograph shows their float at a local carnival.

and so began the Guild's story. The following year the number of shows increased to four, each growing in classes and entries as new residents joined the Guild from expanding Elm Park.

Four shows were planned for 1939 but only three took place. The autumn show was held on 2nd of September and the next day, 3rd September, War was declared. Although a token show was held on 6th July 1940, the Guild went into temporary retirement for the rest of the conflict.

It was reformed and renamed the Elm Park Horticultural Guild in 1948, holding its summer show in Benhurst School on 24th July. During the 1950's all the shows were held in the Constitutional Hall, Elm Park. Since 1961 all the shows have been held in the Assembly Hall. Between 1961 and 1976 the Guild held eight flowers shows a year, but this has decreased to four due to a lack of many specialist growers and exhibitors.

Trading secretary of the Elm Park Horticultural Guild, Fernly Goodanew, with unknown girl and prize winning marrow.

Unfortunately many local horticultural societies such as Upminster and Squirrels Heath have seen a steady decline in both members and exhibitors and no longer hold flower shows. The Elm Park Horticultural Guild is still going strong and also offers other events for its members and has a busy social diary. It organises coach outings to various famous gardens and places of interest, as well as trips to theatres and other places. The Guild also holds floral demonstrations and other social events.

It has well stocked trading huts which are open most Sunday mornings from which composts, fertilizers, canes, trays, etc. are sold to members at reasonable prices. The huts are situated at the side of Elm Park Library in St. Nicholas Avenue. The Elm Park Horticultural Guild is still one of the largest gardening clubs or societies in the country with 1,500 households as paid up members (according to 2007 figures).

We like to think that we are more than just a horticultural guild. We have been an integral part of the community for over 70 years. New members are always welcomed at the trading huts any Sunday morning.

Jean Franklin remembers the Elm Park Horticultural Guild:

My parents joined the Guild in 1945 and were on the committee. My father was Trading Secretary and had a trading hut on the corner of Maybank and South End Road. Previously to that, I remember the fertilisers and other gardening requirements being sold from two mid-terrace houses in Woburn Avenue. Customers walked through the houses into the back gardens to buy the products. My Mum had managed an allotment in Devon when we were evacuated so it was natural to grow our own vegetables back in Elm Park. We had one of the allotments that were on the corner of South End Road and Maybank Avenue. My Dad grew lovely rhubarb that we sold for 2d a pound. Later the hut moved to the British Legion site and then to the present site next to the library. My father, Fernly Goodanew, was the first life member of the Guild in honour of all his services.

On show days, as most people didn't have cars, they brought their produce to the Assembly Hall (or the Constitutional Hall) by home-made wheelbarrows. My mother was in charge of the Homecraft and Handicraft sections and made marvellous cream horns. Mrs Smith made fancy cakes shaped like treasure chests with chocolate money falling out! At home we made our own spiced vinegar for the picked onions (the smell hung around for days.) Mum arranged the onions in straight lines in the jars with a knitting needle. We always had home made jam and bottled gooseberries. Handicrafts included knitted Fairisle pullovers, felt tea cosies shaped like cottages, beautiful embroideries, knitted cardigans and toys.

Children's categories included floating flower heads, growing carrot tops, arranging coloured leaves.

Commemorative show catalogue for the Horticulaural Guild's 60th year.

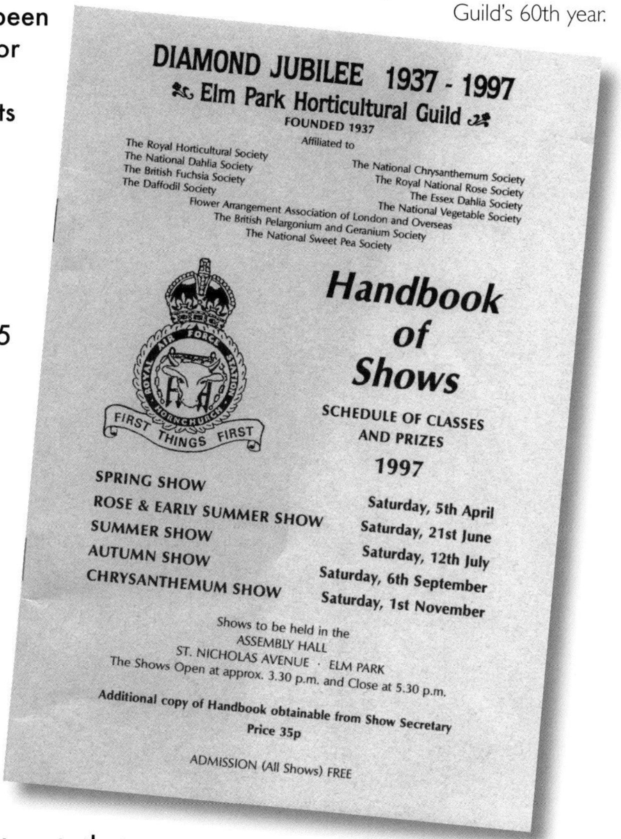

DIAMOND JUBILEE 1937 - 1997
Elm Park Horticultural Guild
FOUNDED 1937

Affiliated to

The Royal Horticultural Society
The National Dahlia Society
The British Fuchsia Society
The Daffodil Society

The National Chrysanthemum Society
The Royal National Rose Society
The Essex Dahlia Society
The National Vegetable Society

Flower Arrangement Association of London and Overseas
The British Pelargonium and Geranium Society
The National Sweet Pea Society

FIRST THINGS FIRST

Handbook of Shows

SCHEDULE OF CLASSES AND PRIZES
1997

SPRING SHOW
ROSE & EARLY SUMMER SHOW
SUMMER SHOW
AUTUMN SHOW
CHRYSANTHEMUM SHOW

Saturday, 5th April
Saturday, 21st June
Saturday, 12th July
Saturday, 6th September
Saturday, 1st November

Shows to be held in the
ASSEMBLY HALL
ST. NICHOLAS AVENUE · ELM PARK
The Shows Open at approx. 3.30 p.m. and Close at 5.30 p.m.

Additional copy of Handbook obtainable from Show Secretary
Price 35p

ADMISSION (All Shows) FREE

What interesting outings we had, to Kew Gardens, Whipsnade Zoo, Spalding tulip fields. Midweek outings for the women included trips to Paynes Poppets (we all enjoyed the free samples of these chocolate coated nuts) Boots in Nottingham, and Stork Margarine in Tilbury. We also had great socials in the Assembly Hall. One of my proudest moments was in 1976 when I won the Goodanew Challenge Shield, which had been donated by my parents.

THE RED CROSS

Jean Franklin recalls the Red Cross Society at Ayloff School:

My sister and I joined the Red Cross junior section in the early 1950's. We learned how to dress bandages, especially difficult ones like those on heads, elbows and knees. We learned how to look after frail people in their own homes and how to cook tempting meals. There was another group who had their headquarters at Roneo Corner and we would have competitions, for example who could make 'hospital beds' the quickest. We passed exams. There was an adult group who would attend fetes and we would go and help too. Eventually a Red Cross building was erected on the corner of Maybank Avenue and the South End Road (now known as Carries Hall). Miss Smithson was the Commandant and after many years service she received the MBE in 2005. My sister was so interested that she became a nurse, doing her training at Oldchurch Hospital.

Brenda Goodanew in her Red Cross uniform

THE WOODCRAFT FOLK

This group met in the Co-op hall and the children wore green shirts. Meetings were inspired by the ideals of Ernest Thompson Seton, an influential writer and naturalist during the 1920's. Children worked in a Co-operative way for badges and learnt about living in the open air, with games, drama, discussions and projects.

Elm Park Co-operative Youth Club

Howard Moss remembers:

> I started going to the Woodcraft folk when I was about six, which would be in 1950. There were about 30 to 40 girls and boys and there were two groups 6-11 years and 11-15 years. It was really ahead of its time as equality between the sexes and between the children and adults was paramount. I left in 1959 but funnily enough came back to run the group with my wife Val in 1970. It was hard work, but fun organising non competitive games, drama and dancing. Every weekend we had outdoor activities like going to camp or the Stubbers Outdoor Pursuits Centre. We

packed it up in 1975 and the group became absorbed into the larger Dagenham group, to which it was affiliated. I've still got the green shirt though!

THE GUIDES AND SCOUTS

Jean Franklin shares her memories:

My life changed when I joined the 1st St. Nicholas Guides. I just loved it. We were a large company of 40 girls and three Guiders and there was always a waiting list! I was enrolled and have tried to keep my promise for the rest of my life. Our Guide Captain was Miss Barbara Lyon who gave her life to Guiding. Our meetings were on a Friday evening and sometimes we went over the park to practise tracking in the bushes and trees on the other side of the stream. We also had jumble sales, so six of us would pull a large cart round Elm Park collecting jumble. It was very hard work! We did Bob-a-Job, knocking on doors and asking if we could do any chores for a bob (a shilling in old money)

Brownies pictured with other members of St Nicholas Church in 1936 courtesy Brian Cornwell

usually cleaning shoes, weeding gardens, or polishing silver. I remember repairing a large tear in a candlewick bedspread and being paid one shilling and sixpence! On Sundays, after 8am Holy Communion, we would do things like catching a bus to Romford to swim at Mawney Road swimming baths or riding our bikes to Cranham Church and then light fires to cook our breakfast in nearby fields. Barbara taught us to sign on each others' hands and we learnt to make things with soaked willows.

In 1953 Canvey Island flooded and Guides and Scouts from all over Essex were asked to help with cleaning up. We were given train passes to Benfleet Station where we were met by open topped lorries which took us to the homes to be cleaned. The Scouts filled up sandbags to build up the sea wall and we Guides were given buckets, mops, brooms, etc. The whole island was grey and in an awful mess. We stayed in the local school, sleeping on the floor and eating in the school canteen. We went to several camps travelling by removal van, the kit in the back and all us Guides hanging out the back singing! At Saffron Walden deer park we woke in the morning to find that deer had eaten a full sack of potatoes, chewed through the ropes of the flagstaff and the guy lines of the mess tent!

Mike Trevallion remembers the Scouts:

When I was a boy I was a keen on the Cubs and then the Scouts. I first joined the second Elm Park but when the Cub leader was off long term sick I transferred to the first Elm Park at St. Nicholas Church. Whilst I was there the new Scout Hall was built, which we shared with the Brownies and Guides.

My first time under canvas was at Stubbers while still with the second Elm Park. I was eight years old and I never looked back! (My sons had their first camp at the same age but always in a hall). The first summer camp for Scouts that I went to was at Biggin Hill, Kent in about 1955. It was raining the day we set off, raining when we arrived to put up the tents, and still raining when we left early on the Thursday due to flooding and loss of some tents in the gales! Every camp after that was heaven, whether it was a cool week or dampish weekend.

Later I joined the Rover Scouts which had been formed by Stewart Bunyan for the eighteen to twenty years olds. We had quite adventurous activities including trek carting across some pretty rough terrain. We travelled in his old Bedford CA van which amazingly never let us down. Hey-ho good memories.

HARROW LODGE PARK

One thing not originally planned for at Elm Park was a public park for the new residents. However, as part of the planning agreement with Hornchurch Urban District Council, Costain donated 34.86 acres to the Council in 1936, 'for use as a public open space'. Costain made sure to capitalise on this in their sales brochures with a photograph showing **'Football in one of the Playing Fields preserved for all time time for residents of Elm Park'**. In 1937 this land was added to Harrow Lodge Park which had only been started in early 1936 when the Council paid the London County Council £16,250 for the 42 acre Harrow Lodge Farm. This area of the park was often described as **'the Elm Park section'** by Hornchurch Council. Though not exclusively part of Elm Park, Harrow Lodge Park is very much part of the Elm Park story.

In 1937 Harrow Lodge was still in a raw condition. The new Elm Park residents would have still been able to see the barn and stable block of Harrow Lodge, an 18th century building which opened in 1936 as the first public library in Hornchurch. An oak fence was later erected around the park. Football pitches were in use and outbuildings had been adapted for changing rooms but none of the paths were laid and at least one field had just been sown with grass seed.

Harrow Lodge park paddling pool and sandpit in the late forties

Playing on the swings in Harrow Lodge Park

Many of the early plans for this park were delayed by the War when 60 acres of land was used for intensive food production. One happy development of the War years was the paddling pool built in 1944 for the *Holidays at Home* campaign and this remained a popular attraction for many years afterwards. The playground was developed with a major addition of new equipment in 1951. In 1957, three 'box type' swings were added creating the features popularly associated with childhood parks.

The park became a popular centre for sport. In 1947 the first land released from food production was converted into two cricket pitches and during 1948 a disused pit adjoining Rainham Road was filled in and four tennis courts were constructed. An 18-hole miniature golf course was set out in 1952 and a boating lake followed during the years 1954 to 1956. The cricket pavilion was erected in 1960. By the '50s there were netball courts too.

Following the success of a bowling green at Haynes Park another was laid at Harrow Lodge Park on land acquired through compulsory

Roundabout in Harrow Lodge Park play area 1940s

Harrow Lodge Park boating lake before the willow trees were planted

purchase. The park was big enough to accommodate the building of the Hornchurch Swimming Pool, officially opened in 1956. In 1960 a swim would cost 9d for a child and it was possible to hire trunks for 6d. In 1987 the pool was redeveloped as Hornchurch Sports Centre.

Del Ramsey recalls his early days in Harrow Lodge Park:

> There was not a lot of things for kids to do in Elm Park, so I used to spend hours in Harrow Lodge Park, playing football or playing on the pitch and putt golf course with my mates. The golf course was a popular attraction, but, of course, you had to pay to use it. We used to throw some rope over an old oak tree down by the river near the new play area and swing from that. I played football for Elm Park – I remember wearing a green and red

chequered shirt. The changing rooms were situated close to one of the Warren Drive entrances and were also used by the park keepers to store equipment. In those days, there used to be four park keepers who patrolled the park by foot or by bike.

In the summer we had family picnics by the paddling pool. When the new indoor swimming pool opened, I learned to swim a length in three weeks!

After the war Harrow Lodge developed as the main nursery for Hornchurch Urban District Council with the first greenhouses provided in 1947 and heated frames added by 1960. The park included showcase carpet beds outside the swimming pool and a rock garden was established as early as 1948. When the London Borough of Havering was created in 1965 the nursery at Harrow Lodge remained, along with the Romford Borough Council nursery at Bedfords Park.

Elm Park Bowls Club

Government-instigated changes in the management of public parks in the 1980s saw the end of the Council's nurseries.

One major development within the park was the Garden for the Blind, opened on 22nd July 1961. This garden had wider pathways and aromatic plants with a centrepiece dolphin fountain creating sound for visitors. Though the garden declined over time, it has been revived through the efforts of volunteers and the Secret Garden, complete with Braille labelling and fragrant flowers, came second in the Havering in Bloom Best Community Garden category in 2006.

Harrow Lodge Park now covers more than 120 acres and remains a popular place for residents of Elm Park to enjoy the playgrounds, sports facilities, planting and the wildlife of the Site of Importance for Nature Conservation found bordering the River Ravensbourne as well as the small wooded areas and less intensively managed parts of the park.

THE WAR YEARS

We saw a low flying aircraft, which we thought was one of ours, till it started firing and we all rushed indoors. After the war, when Dad was redecorating the bathroom, he dug two or three machine gun bullets out of the ceiling.

Joan Shoush…memories of Lancaster Drive

At the outbreak of War, house-building on the estate stopped, as resources were focused on the War effort. There was confusion about how safe the area was. Whilst some people fled their homes, fearing raids on the nearby RAF Hornchurch, others evacuated to Elm Park to escape the bombing raids over London. Because so many homes stood empty, police would patrol the streets on their bicycles and even challenge people coming out of their own homes asking them to account for their presence there. A large public air raid shelter was built on what is now Tadworth Parade. Near to this shelter stood a large round water reservoir which was to be used as an emergency water supply. This tank, as well as several others scattered around Elm Park, was fed from the water supply on Costain's yard by a black water pipe that snaked through Elm Park. This emergency water supply was maintained by the Auxiliary Fire Service (AFS) for tackling fires caused by the bombing.

Anti tank barriers appeared either side of the railway station. An Air Raid Precaution (ARP) hut stood in Coronation Drive, which housed a large supply of gas masks. South End Road was blocked off at the junction of Wood Lane and the perimeter of the aerodrome was a mass of barbed wire as security intensified around RAF Hornchurch. A lot of people dug up their back gardens in order to erect an Anderson shelter. Here they would keep emergency supplies of food and drink, and blankets to keep warm. As the shelter was covered with earth to help absorb shocks from the bombs, many people successfully grew vegetables, like marrows for example, on the top of them. These shelters generally proved unpopular for, even with the use of pumps, they had a tendency to flood. Later, the Morrison shelter proved more useful as it was designed to be used indoors. It consisted of a reinforced metal cage with a steel-plate top that could be erected anywhere. It was often placed in the living room and doubled as a table. Many people simply chose to hide under the stairs!

People were instructed to criss-cross brown sticky paper on all their windows to stop them shattering in the bomb blasts and hang black out curtains at all windows. This was to prevent enemy bombers spotting the lights of a town and thus have a target for their bombs. All the street lamps were turned off and people had to learn to find their way around in the dark, often bumping into posts and trees and falling down kerbs. To help the situation kerbs and posts had white stripes painted on them but accidents were still common. To enforce these war-time regulations the ARP wardens patrolled the streets. Everyone was issued with identity papers and a gas mask, which had to be carried at all times. Food and clothing became scarcer and so were rationed and people were urged to 'Dig for Victory' and 'Make do and Mend'.

High explosives demolished this Anderson shelter in South End Road, backing onto Ayloff school. 31st August 1940

Allotments in front of the original St Nicholas Church.

Elm Park residents responded enthusiastically and dug up their ornamental flower beds to grow vegetables and learnt how to turn parachute silk into underwear. Any spare plot of land was converted into allotments and many people have fond memories of time spent on these plots.

Edna Bono enjoyed her family's allotment:

> My Dad had an allotment in Abbs Cross Lane (where the secondary school now stands) Money was tight but everyone ate healthily. We grew the basics, like potatoes, cabbages, carrots. It was a treat for us to go and dig up the vegetables or help with the weeding and watering. We kept chickens in our back garden too; the eggs were good to eat or to trade with neighbours for other produce. One day I was collecting the eggs when our cockerel, Joseph, started menacing me and wouldn't let me leave the pen. I was only little, about six years old, and I was very frightened. I screamed and shouted for Mum who took ages to hear me. But when she did hear me she came running round the side of the house with the copper stick in her hand and really gave that Joseph what for! Mum then turned round and gave me what for!

Evelyn Holloway also remembers her Dad's allotment:

> We were all told to grow more food and my Dad had an allotment where St Alban's church now stands. I carried buckets of water for the celery he grew. We also collected manure left by the horses pulling the carts that delivered bread, milk and greengrocery. We were rationed for most foods and even sweets. I had extra clothing coupons because I had big feet!

Joan Shoush recalls Sunday 3rd September, 1939, the day war broke out:

I heard a strange loud wailing noise. My mother was upstairs and she came rushing down so fast that she fell down the last few steps. I remember her lying on the floor. My older sister was at church and family tradition has it that all the mothers rushed to the church to collect their children only to find that the vicar had locked the door and was saying prayers whilst all the mothers hammered on the door clamouring to get in. Later on we became more blasé and we waited till we heard the Tannoy telling the pilots to get into their planes and then we knew that it was time to get into our shelter!

When I had to post a letter to my father I was always very careful to hold the envelope with the address against my coat in case an enemy agent should read it and know where my father's ship was. Clothing was a problem as it was rationed as well as food. I inherited someone's buttoned gaiters, which I hated because they were very old fashioned even then. But as boots were difficult to buy I was made to wear them in the winter to keep me warm.

Elm Park Library exhibition comments book 1995:

We were one of only two families left in our part of Maybank Avenue because we were 'barbed-wired' in as part of the aerodrome. This meant that no coalman or milkman could get to us and we had to go down to the opening at the bottom of the road to collect our milk and coal. We could see Spitfires shot at and when a bomb dropped right in our garden the aircrews came to see if we were all right.

Ena Risby remembers September 1940

One day during the Battle of Britain my mother, two brothers and myself and the milkman (who had covered his horse's head with a sack and left him outside on the road) were all in our Anderson shelter. I can remember us all holding our hands over our ears and staring at each other as the sacking over the shelter door blew backwards and forwards with the turmoil that was going on outside. When the air raid was over we came out of the shelter and there was devastation all around. Over at the RAF Hornchurch camp, huts were on fire and there was smoke everywhere. There were a lot of airmen and WAAFs killed on that awful day.

Later Havering paid its own tribute to the heroes of RAF Hornchurch by naming a group of local roads after some of the pilots who took part in the Battle of Britain.

A pair of Villette houses damaged by bombs

Damage caused by the first bomb to fall on Elm Park on 26th August 1940. High explosives demolished this house, 55, Benhurst Avenue

Houses on the corner of Benhurst Avenue and Beech Close

Morecambe Close, the nearest house to the airfield.

Arbour Way

Elm Park was acutely aware of the dangers of War and a special relationship between those serving in the RAF and the residents of Elm Park was established. Shops, pubs, cafes and clubs all welcomed the pilots and helped to make the lives of those putting their lives at risk more bearable.

Sheila Fry remembers her Mum's café:

My Mother, Lillian Strellis, owned the Elm Park Café in 1939 and throughout the war. I worked there, very long hours from 6am to midnight, but I loved it. We kept open to provide hot meals for the airmen from RAF Hornchurch who could come off duty any time of day or night. I met lots of airmen of all nationalities, Canadian, New Zealanders, and Americans. They were all good natured, laughing young men. I also saw some of the famous names of aviation history, Douglas Bader, Paddy Finucane, and 'Sailor' Malan.

Mum was an excellent cook and could make nourishing meals from next to nothing, just a little meat, vegetables and dumplings. She also made tasty plum duff and jam roly poly puddings. Sometimes Phil, the manager at Delin's, would say 'I've got a case of eggs for you.' Then Mum would put 'Camouflage' on the menu for the aircrews. For 1/6d you had a fried egg hidden (or camouflaged) under a huge pile of chips served with bread and butter and a cup of tea. This stopped anyone else spotting the coveted egg (a rare war time treat) especially an inspector! Usually the airmen 'put it on the slate' that is, had it on credit and then paid the bill at the end of the week. Sadly, all too often, the slate was wiped clean because the airman had been killed on active service.

Al Fulcher remembers the day his school was saved from tragic devastation:

> I'll never forget the day, Wednesday March 24th 1943, when I was at school (Suttons Secondary School). My class was having a gardening lesson and we were weeding the flower beds surrounding the school when suddenly a Spitfire aircraft appeared to be in trouble. It crash-landed on our playground. The pilot had seemed to be trying to land on our playing fields but went too far and overturned on the playground, breaking in half. The pilot was killed. He was an American called Raimond Sanders Draper aged 25. Later his parents came to our school to receive the thanks of students, teachers and parents. He gave his life to avoid hitting the school and the classrooms with all the children inside them.

Portrait of Raimund Sanders Draper which hangs in the school which later took his name

The Romford Times report mentions broken school windows and three boys slightly injured by flying glass. At the time of the crash there were about a thousand children in the school, many of whom dived under their desks as they heard the airplane come down. The gardening class and their teacher, Mr Meads, threw down their forks and scattered for cover, as the plane bounced on the playing fields and came to rest about two yards from the windows of a classroom. A quarter of an hour later would have been playtime, when the playground would have been filled with children. After the crash the headmaster assembled all the children in the hall but they were allowed home for dinner. The school day resumed in the afternoon as usual.

Peter Moss also remembers air raids in 1943:

> We'd moved back to Elm Park and I started at Ayloff School.
> After the first couple of occasions I had to walk there by myself (I
> was five) about a quarter of a mile, and home for dinner too! On
> the way to school I had to pass an AA (anti aircraft) site set up
> in the front garden of the corner house of South End Road and
> Farm Way. A good number of times we had air raid warnings for
> real and I recall running for the shelter with the guns firing and
> the bombs dropping. Once I stopped to do up my shoelace and
> the teacher went mad at me, telling me to keep running. When
> we got to the shelters, they were brick surface ones with concrete
> roofs, we were organised into singing groups, to drown out the
> noise. I was happy at this school but don't think that I learned
> much. Classes had 50 pupils and we played a lot of games. We
> boys collected shrapnel and swapped pieces from our tins. From
> the school playing field we'd watch the steam trains go by with
> their sticky taped windows. Several houses in Elm Farm Road had
> been bombed and we children played in the rubble. A couple of
> times during the war we went down to the village hall in Elm Park
> to the communal kitchen/restaurant.

From 1941 the government encouraged local authorities to set up British or
'Civic' Restaurants. People were able to eat a cheap, convenient three course
meal for 9d. Although open to all, British Restaurants mainly catered for office
and factory workers and they were similar in many ways to a works canteen.

Al Fulcher remembers preparations for D-Day:

> There were thousands of troop carrier vehicles, jeeps, trailers
> with guns on them, small utility vehicles and many other war
> vehicles, USA and British army troops and RAF personnel were
> all getting ready for D day landings. They parked on every road,
> on the 'even number' side. The troops slept and were fed at the
> aerodrome. They had guards looking after the vehicles during
> the night and many residents would give them tea or coffee
> and snacks. Then after several days they were all gone and
> transported to the ships that would take them across to France.
> It was strange knowing that a lot of them that we had seen and
> spoken to would never return. They gave their lives to bring the
> beginning of peace once more to the world.

Peter Moss also remembers D-Day preparations:

> One day Mother said we should go out and we went to Maybank
> Avenue and we stopped by the barbed wire across the road.
> All of a sudden my Father was there, talking to us, on the other
> side of the wire. We were warned not to ask questions. I learned
> later he was at RAF Hornchurch on a training course. Several

days later, Elm Farm Road was full of American army vehicles. Their personnel used to start up the jeeps and lorries early every morning then shut them down after half an hour or so. We got on well with these young men and played cricket using their fuel cans as the wicket. They thought the rules strange because I think they thought they were playing baseball. They were there for two or three weeks, then the great day came, one night there was a seemingly endless roar of aircraft going overhead, eastwards. We looked out of Mum's bedroom window and I could see aircraft, with their invasion stripes, flying low, many with gliders attached, going over. The next morning the vehicles had gone and I've often wondered how those lads got on in France.

Brian Cornwell remembers the V1s:

On 6th August 1944 about 3.30am I remember houses at the back of us in St Andrews Avenue being struck by a doodlebug. My parents watched the bomb coming towards us after it passed over the Officers Mess on RAF Hornchurch. We all took cover in the Morrison Shelter in the front room. In our house the blast from the bomb blew a door from its hinges, damaged the internal lounge wall, and blew the lid off the piano! Glass from the windows was everywhere and Mother lay newspaper on the floor to protect our feet from shards of glass. Tiles were ripped from our roof but that was nothing compared to the four houses in St Andrews Avenue that had to be demolished and fifteen other houses severely damaged. Two people were killed. The RAF maintained a Repair Unit which came to help with the initial clearing up. We were then evacuated to a friend's house in Ambleside Avenue, and then to an empty property in Maybank Avenue. We had the ground floor and another family had the

Warren Drive Victory Committee in the playground at Benhurst School

first floor and we had to share the kitchen and bathroom. After the War we used to play on the bomb damaged site.

After the war many streets clubbed together to give everyone, but particularly the children, a party to remember. Although food was scarce everyone did their utmost to provide sandwiches and cakes, and fun in the form of fancy dress competitions and games. However no one forgot that many would not return from the war.

VJ Party in Warren Drive

VE Party in the Reid family's back garden

VJ Party held in 1946 on ground at the Costain
Estate Office in Coronation Drive.

R.A.F. HORNCHURCH

William Leefe Robinson VC

No account of the War years would be complete without including a mention of the local aerodrome, which opened as RFC Sutton's Farm in 1915 to combat the threat of Zeppelins. In September 1916 William Leefe Robinson flew from Sutton's Farm and became the first man to shoot down a German Zeppelin over England, for which he was awarded a VC. Frederick Sowery and William Tempest also shot down Zeppelins for which they were awarded the DSO. The aerodrome was briefly restored to Thomas Crawford, the farmer owner, between 1920 and 1924 when it was once again requisitioned by the RAF as an aerodrome.

The airfield was small but in an ideal location to defend the approach to London. During the Second World War RAF Hornchurch was a fighter station and squadrons from Hornchurch played a key role in the Battle of Britain. Hornchurch also controlled two satellite airfields and it became the most renowned Spitfire station in Fighter Command. 54 Squadron destroyed the most Luftwaffe aircraft during the Battle of Britain and Eric Lock of 41 Squadron had the most individual hits.

Gloster planes at the 1937 RAF Hornchurch open day

Famous names from aviation history flew from Hornchurch including Douglas Bader, Walter Beaumont, George Bennions, Cecil Bouchier, Harry Broadhurst, Brian Carbury, Alan Deere, George Denholme, and Derek Dowding. Paddy Finucane, Petrus Hugo, Donald Kingaby, James Leathart, Eric Lock, 'Sailor' Malan, John Mungo-Park, Keith Park, Peter Simpson, Alfred Sarre, Frederick Sowery, Gerald Stapleton, Robert Stanford Tuck to name but a few. As Winston Churchill famously said: "Never in the field of human conflict has so much been owed by so many to so few."

Ken Gibson recalls:

RAF Hornchurch scramble

There's a famous story of how Fighter Pilot Alan Deere crash landed near Dunkirk after a run in with a Dornier 17. After his wounds were dressed he managed to get to Dunkirk where he got a place on a Navy destroyer to Dover. From there he took a train to Charing Cross and then District Line train to Elm Park station, just as if he was an ordinary commuter. After explaining himself to the ticket inspector he was waved through and the next day he rejoined his squadron at RAF Catterick for rest and recuperation. That's the calibre of men that fought from RAF Hornchurch.

Ted Exall gave a talk at Rainham Library in 1991 and recalled:

Don't forget we're talking about a time when anything south of the Thames was considered enemy territory. I've a letter here from Air Commodore James Leathart, where he tells the following story about a bombing take off. It was the only time he took off without permission, which was a heinous sin to commit. Leathart was sitting in the cockpit of his Spitfire when there was a raid on RAF Hornchurch. He could see a German bomber formation approaching. He told the ops room but they couldn't see anything so he gave the order to take off! The German bombs dropped where he had been waiting. Sergeant Davis was blown over the dirty little river by the airfield and landed in a field. Well, he wasn't going to swim home was he? So Davis got a taxi for the two or three mile round trip back to camp and they refused to pay the fare! Leathart wrote and complained about this shabby treatment and eventually the War Office paid up and the station accountant was sacked!

41 Squadron at RAF Hornchurch

Eileen Wilson recalls:

I can remember riding my bike from home along the South End Road past the Hornchurch Aerodrome. All along the road were huge barricades of barbed wire on either side with warning signs saying 'Beware of Low Flying Aircraft.' Although the War was over by then the aerodrome was still in use for the training of air force cadets and it was a common sight to see the lads out and about. For some reason the Good Intent pub was out of bounds to the cadets, and they used to come to the Elm Park Hotel where regular dances were held in what is now the Stardust Ballroom.

After the war RAF Hornchurch became an officer selection centre and Ronnie Corbett, the comedian, and Edward Hardwicke the actor were stationed there. Ronnie refers to his time there in his autobiography "High Hopes." The airfield closed in June 1962.

Unveiling of the RAF Hornchurch memorial by Air Chief Marshal Sir Harry Broadhurst 5th July 1983

SHOPS AND SHOPPING

Costain's promotional brochure of around 1935 claimed:

There is nothing for the home, the table, or the personal wants of residents that Elm Park shops cannot supply.

Elm Park started out with a few essential shops that supplied basic needs. There were several dairies, Hitchmans, the Co-op, and United Dairies; Sam Weller who sold radios and bicycles and was known for his accumulator radios, Hollick the newsagent and post office and the Grays Co-op store. However, many of the shops remained empty for some time.

1937 corner of Elm Park Broadway and Elm Park Avenue

By the late 1930's Elm Park had the following: Wright the corn chandlers, the Grays Co-op department store (which sold furniture, carpets and textiles) and Woolworth. There were Levine and Allen chemists, Beilters and Barton bakers, Finlay and Tuck Box tobacconists, Hollick newsagent, Castle Sports who sold bikes radios and accessories, Wellands, Goodwoods, Delins, Perks, Tesco and Funnels grocers, Brigden and Middleton fishmonger and fried fish shop. There was Dolly's and Jan's for dresses and women's wear. Meyers, Spicers and Knights supplied greengrocery and Bata, Tru-Form, Turner and Fortress sold shoes. Leonards and Stevens were butchers and Treasure House sold wool and needle crafts. There was a café. There was a hardware store called Dennis and if you walked through Finlay's the tobacconists you found a barbers at the back of the shop.

Ken Coe remembers:

> Many of the shops stayed vacant for some time, probably because of the uncertainty of the times. There were three or four empty shops in the parade where the wedding dress shop now is. These were used for storage, possibly the boxes belonged to one of the other shopkeepers or the builders. After the war three of the shops were converted to make the National Nursery. Many of the shopkeepers traded in Elm Park for years and were well known locally.

Welcome to Elm Park , looking up The Broadway

Ken Daley remembers the nursery:

> It was in St Nicholas Avenue and it had a strange boarded up
> front with an inset door with very high windows, so you couldn't
> look out into the street. The walls were painted green half way up
> the walls and then cream. Although it was drab inside my brother
> and I loved it there. We used to go from 1945, while our Mum
> was at work and our older brothers and sisters were at school.
> There always seemed to be lots of toys and lots to do. Of course,
> at home we had very few toys because of the war. My most vivid
> memory is of two staff, pretty ginger-haired sisters called Miss
> Gregory. They made our days there great fun until it was time for
> us to go to school.

Vera Cornwell remembers:

> Wright's the corn chandlers was an interesting old shop. It always
> seemed old fashioned even when it was new. I used to go in there
> and buy dog biscuits. There was a wooden floor and wooden
> counters and everything was stored in big sacks. There was
> always a beautiful smell, that's what I remember the most about it.

Margaret Hoepelman loved buying butter:

> I used to love going to the United Dairies because I was
> fascinated with the way they served the butter. There would be
> a massive mound of the stuff and they'd break off a chunk of
> butter and bash it into shape with wooden butter pats. When it
> was done to the staff's satisfaction a rose was stamped on the
> top and the whole pat wrapped in wax paper. It was a real skill
> serving that butter!

Elm Park Library exhibition comments book 1995

> Treasure House had a Dolls' Hospital where you could get your
> doll repaired. In the sweet shop we bought gobstoppers, two for
> ha'penny or four blackjacks for a ha'penny.

> The bakers had a bread slicing machine. As children we used to
> eat slices of bread when carrying it home. We were registered at
> Perks the grocers during the war.

> Before the public library opened I used to visit the Wych Elm
> Library near the (old) post office. Each book borrowed cost
> 3d (old money) and when you returned the books there was a
> rebate.

Eileen Wilson remembers:

> Another of my memories was of the time before betting was
> legalised (in 1960). Anyone daring enough to place a bet on
> Derby Day or on the Grand National used to furtively make their
> way to the alleyway at the back of the Halifax Building Society.
> There was an old disused railway carriage alongside the railway
> where the illegal betting took place. Naturally no receipts were
> given but you could give an anonymous name for claims if you
> were a lucky winner! You were always on the look out for any
> policemen but I don't remember anyone ever getting caught.

CHAIN STORES

Woolworth's was one of the first stores to open in Elm Park, on 27th May 1938.
Photographs of it appear in the early advertising brochures. The bright red
fascia and gold lettering, F. W. Woolworth & Co shone proudly over the awning
pulled down to protect the window display. Woolworth's always sold a wide
variety of goods but will be best remembered for its pick and mix sweets.

Freda Gill thinks of Woolworth's with affection:

> I used to love Woolworth's. When I was young and I'd got no
> money I could wander round the store and think: "When I've

A typical Woolworth interior

saved up enough I could buy that Alice band or that rope of 'pearls', or I'd love that 'diamond' ring". There were wooden floors, side counters and island counters all painted maroon, staffed by young women. School leavers loved getting jobs there, especially on jewellery or cosmetics! They wore maroon overalls with no pockets. The price cards were A4 size cream card with a red border held on a metal stand and prices were standard throughout the shop, 3d or 6d! I remember once coming home on the bus from Hornchurch with my Mum. It would have been spring 1945 and we'd been there to report the bomb damage done by a V2 rocket to our house in Rainham. When the bus stopped in Elm Park Avenue just near Woolworth's Mum said: "Quick. they look as if they've got something in," and we had to hurry off the bus to investigate. Mum was always after knicker elastic (which was like gold dust during the war) cottons, needles, hairnets, anything that was usable or swappable. I always carried a ration book with points in it to buy anything that became available. If we didn't need it someone else would want it! One of my best Woolworth's buys was just after the war and they got in some crocus bulbs. Now you've got to remember our countryside was all given over to food production and poor Holland had been occupied. So up till then we had to beg, borrow or steal plants and seeds. We were only allowed to buy five bulbs and they cost me 3d. We planted them in the front garden and watched those bulbs like hawks and when they came up they were all yellow. But we had years of pleasure from them.

Sadly this store closed in January 2009 after over 70 years trading in Elm Park.

Above: Elm Park Avenue looking towards Woolworth.

View looking along Elm Parade, with The Elm Park Hotel on the right. c. 1954

Vera Cornwell remembers the Co-op:

Grays Co-op was on the corner of the Broadway and Elm Park Avenue. Everyone who shopped there had a divi-number, I can still remember mine, and we had to tell this number to the shopkeeper when we paid. Every now and again we got our dividend back, a rebate of money for being a good customer. The Co-op was several different shops in a block, like a department store. There was a grocers, greengrocers, butchers, drapers, a chemist and a furniture department. You had to queue at each individual counter for your shopping. In the haberdashery department was a cashier's kiosk. When it was time to pay for your shopping the money was put into a metal tube and the lid screwed on. The tube was connected to a system of wires, across the ceiling of the shop from all directions to the cashier's booth at the front corner of the shop. The cashier sat inside collecting the payments and issuing change. Customers waited at the counter and watched their money whiz along the ceiling and then their change and receipt come whizzing back to them.

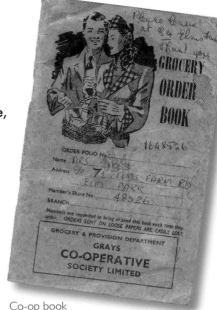

Co-op book

Tom Daley's Co-op memories

In 1962 I worked for the Grays Co-op bakers in Elm Park. It was situated behind the store down a back entrance. A lorry delivered the bread and cakes at 6.30am. They were for the baker's shop and for the six rounds men. Each man had an electric push cart and this had to be loaded up with the bread and cakes before we started work. The cart had to be pushed over the hill to our route, which for me, were the streets around Maybank Avenue and Lancaster Drive. We carried the bread and cakes to the door in a big basket to tempt the customer to buy more. If any one was out when we called, we would put their bread in a paper bag and hang it from the letter box. On Good Friday we made a special delivery of hot cross buns. People used to laugh at the signs on the back of the barrow. On one side it said 'Use your loaf' and on the other 'Get your crumpets here.' I was often asked for stale loaves to make bread pudding because it was sold at half price. We were out in all weathers, rain or shine. If it was raining my baker's boy liked to hitch a ride back to the depot inside the barrow to keep dry. Snow was always a problem: once I was the only baker to make it through the snow!

Several of the new emerging multiple chain stores opened shops in Elm Park including a small Tesco, Boot's the chemist and in the station foyer, W.H. Smith's. The June 1938 Romford and Hornchurch Telephone List and Traders Directory lists Tesco Stores Ltd, 21 The Broadway where Lloyd's Bank now stands. During the 1930's Jack Cohen, co founder of Tescos, was moving away from market trading and into developing suburban sites. The first conventional shop was in Green Lane, Becontree. By 1939 he had over a hundred small shops in the London area.

Ken Daley remembers:

> My first job in 1957 was in Tesco on the hill leading up to Elm Park station. Supermarkets were a very new, American idea and Tesco was one of the first self service shops in the area. Once inside the shop you picked up a basket and chose your shopping as you went along. Prices were on the shelves not on the goods themselves. At the back of the shop was the bacon counter where bacon and ham and cheese were cut up in the traditional way. The price was written on the bag for the cashier. She sat at a till near the door. She had a list of all the prices and looked up each item before entering it up on the till. Luckily shops didn't have such a great variety of goods then! There was the manager, his wife the cashier, Bernard on the bacon counter and three of us lads to sort out deliveries and fill the shelves. We worked down in a huge basement as big as the shop above. Deliveries were unpacked and stacked on the shelves exactly the same as the store. There was a counter

Elm Park Avenue late fifties.

ELM PARK AVENUE, ELM PARK.

where we used to cut up the cheese, wrap it in cellophane and stick on a price ticket, the beginnings of pre packed food. The cheese was delivered in huge rounds. The rind was cut off with wire cutters and cut into small pieces. We always managed to get enough odd pieces for our lunchtime rolls. We had to take everything up steep stairs in the wire baskets. If there was a pretty girl in the shop we all suddenly found a basket of goods to be taken up.

Tom the knife grinder in Northwood Avenue

STREET TRADERS

As well as the local shops, Elm Park residents had a number of street traders who called at the door. In addition to the milk and bread deliveries, regular callers were the oilman (with paraffin for heaters), coal man, knife grinder, a greengrocer and ice cream sellers. On Sunday mornings a seafood vendor would tour the streets and people treated themselves to winkles, cockles, prawns or whelks for their Sunday tea. Other callers included the insurance agent, the tallyman (who sold goods on credit then called regularly for payment), the window cleaner and the chimney sweep.

ELM PARK LIBRARY exhibition comments book 1995:

I remember my father walking behind the United Dairy milkman (with his horse and cart) carrying a bucket and shovel. He was a keen gardener and he thought there was nothing like horse manure for roses!

We lived in a mid terrace house in St. Andrews Avenue and I can remember when the coal man arrived, my mother rushing up the hallway pulling the carpet runner up as she went in case any coal was spilled. She would be very annoyed if the coal was wet.

You could choose your meat in the shop and were given a raffle ticket. The butcher then stored the meat until Saturday. This was in the days when people didn't have fridges or freezers at home. You could either collect the meat yourself, handing over your raffle ticket, or have it delivered at home.

Terry Malby remembers:

Dickie Bird's ice cream van would have a regular pitch in Wood Lane at about 7.30pm each night. The van would sell sweets, papers, and cigarettes as well as ice cream. This went on for over two decades during 1950's to 1970's. Barton's the bakers called daily with a wicker basket of bread and cakes. The milkman came every day at 5am! It was probably the Co-op as Mum was keen to collect points towards the dividend. A shoe repair man visited regularly and would mend heels and soles on your doorstep. A knife grinder also came round. My favourite was the rag and bone man. He rang a bell as he toured the streets. If you gave him something he might give you a goldfish, or money, or sweets, depending on what he thought your donation worth.

THE BELGIAN

Along the Upper Rainham Road was a general store. It was run by Antoine Vandenabeele, a well known local character who was simply known as the Belgian or the King of the Belgians. He lived in an old Victorian style house backing on to the Chase. This eccentric man claimed that he was the illegitimate son of the King of the Belgians. From his home he ran a small shop which sold amongst other things milk, bread, dried goods, sweets and vegetables.

Mavis Darby remembers going for sweets:

Apart from the Chase there was one other thing that stayed in my mind from childhood and that was a house that was referred to locally as The Belgian's. Turning left as you leave Laburnum Avenue and walking down the hill towards Elm Park there was an isolated house on the right hand side of Rainham Road where the downstairs was turned into a sweet shop. All the local children used the shop, as it was the only sweet shop in the area. There was never any conversation with the owner. You just pointed to what you wanted and proffered the money. This would have been pre war experience as, with rationing, eating sweets became a bit of a luxury.

Mr Vandenabeele built an extension to the front of his house and there were barns and out buildings on the site. He would allow travellers to camp in his fields and from there they would go round the Elm Park Estate selling heather and wooden clothes pegs. Also a travelling circus would use his fields and the ring master was 'Mr. Pastry' (the actor Richard Hearn.) The front of this square brick built house was dominated by a large niche over the doorway where a painted statue of the Virgin Mary stood. Local people remember the statue well but one day it disappeared, presumably stolen. The haulage company Pinch and Co took over the site and used the land to store their heavy plant machinery and their distinctive bottle green and white lorries. The house was used as offices. This was during 1960's at the time of the building of The Glens housing estate. Eventually, the site was sold off, quite a lot of landfill work had to be done and the land was allowed to settle. The present Maylands Health Centre is built on the site.

WARTIME SHOPPING

After the outbreak of World War Two, shopping patterns had to change. Rationing was introduced for food and clothing in 1940 and only ended in 1954. Families had to register with one supplier and everyone had a ration book. A 'points' scheme was introduced for unrationed food. Most people ate less meat, fat, sugar, and increased their intake of vegetables. Many people were better fed during the war than previously due to a more healthy diet. Children born during the war were on average taller and heavier than children born before the war. The local Welfare Clinic in Abbs Cross Lane dispensed cod liver oil, orange juice and milk to young children, as well as to expectant and nursing mothers. Non essential food such as bananas and oranges disappeared from the shelves and a whole generation of children grew up not knowing how to eat them.

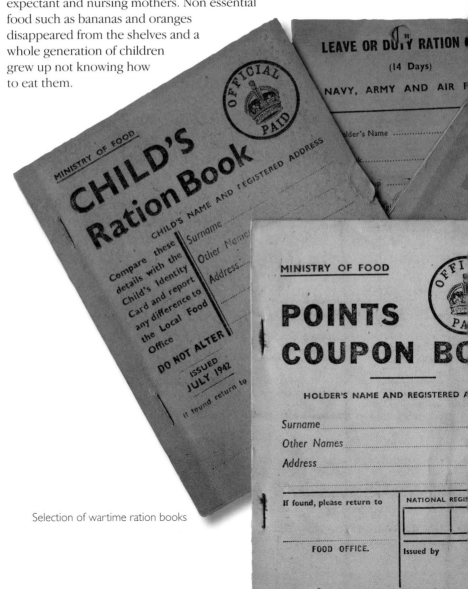

Selection of wartime ration books

Joan Shoush remembers:

I can still remember the thrill of getting an orange to eat but not knowing that you had to peel it first. My cousin refused to eat that strange thing she'd been given, a banana!

Ken Coe recalls:

Everyone had to be registered at the shop of their choice and my Mother registered at the Grays Co-op to collect her rations. She preferred the Grays Co-op because they paid the best dividend, often as high as 3/9d when the London Co-op only paid out 1/9d per quarter. Even after the war food was on ration and didn't end until 1954. In fact bread was first rationed in 1946. I remember meeting a friend by chance outside the shops one day when I was home on leave from the forces. She gave me her bread ration so that we could buy some cakes to share, a rare luxury in those days!

Mrs Crouch remembers:

Food was scarce. We were only allowed 2oz of cheese. My Mother had to queue for everything. To make sure we had enough food we kept chickens. We had ducks on a pond in the back garden, and we kept rabbits as well for food. We grew all our own vegetables, enough to feed us and the animals. All our neighbours did the same. If there was anything over we shared with each other. We managed on what we grew and there was never any waste. My favourite shop in Elm Park was the Tuck Box where we got our sweet rations.

Pete Lines remembers the war time shops for a different reason:

During the war my Mum worked in one of the deep basements that ran under several of the shops on the hill. She made brass parts for the M.O.D. as part of the War effort and we used to joke that Mum made the bullets and Dad fired them because he was fighting abroad. After the war she continued to work there making press out parts for metal toys until the factory relocated in the early 1950s.

POST WAR SHOPS

Tadworth Parade as the final coat of paint is applied, mid fifties

End block of Tadworth Parade Shops in Maylands Avenue

inutes of Hornchurch Urban District Council from 1953 to 1955 show
various applications for shop fronts and illuminated signs in Tadworth
Parade including Home and Colonial Stores, Dewhurst Butchers, West
Butchers, Goodriches, Blows Electrical, Lema Laundrette, Appleton's Fish Shop,
William Fox Chemist, George's Hobby Stores, Regal fish restaurant and Model
Homes Furnishers Ltd.

In March 1956 a new street on the west side of The Broadway was named
in the Council minutes as Station Parade. A new development of shops and
maisonettes on the east side of the Broadway (where Young's Travel is now) was
to be known as North Parade. In 1956 an application was made to use number
1 North Parade as Barclay's Bank. Messrs G. S. Bowler and Sons applied to use
the rear of the basements of 18/19 and 27/28 The Broadway for the manufacture
of tin strawberry basket handles!

Rosewood Avenue looking towards station before Station Parade shops were built

According to the 1957 Romford telephone directory A.S. Bowen Chemist and M. Hunter ophthalmic optician were trading from Station Parade. Many will remember the seemingly large supermarket Wallis which later traded as International, then Kwik Save, and currently as Nisa Stores. Webbs Garden Supplies, R.G. Coles and Thake's the greengrocers have traded from Station Parade for many years.

Sixties view of Webbs Garden Supplies in Station Parade.

A new parade of shops with maisonettes above opened opposite Woolworth's in 1959 and one of the first shops to open was The Hobby Shop.

1960's postcard depicting Elm Park shopping parades and Harrow Lodge Park

The Hobby Shop remembered by Glenn H. Morgan as "unchanged from when I was a child…still the staff in their blue button-up coats. Airfix models, tiny tins of paint and packs of balsawood were in the window - only the prices had changed, as they no longer had kits at 1s11d (or 9.5p from 1971)!"

POST WAR HOUSING IN ELM PARK

After the War building materials were scarce. Permission for buildings was often granted on a temporary basis such as in January 1947 when the British Legion was granted permission to build a temporary building (to stand for ten years) on land near Maylands Avenue. For private developers such as Costain it was a frustrating time. Local councils were given higher priority to go ahead with their own house building programmes and in May 1947 Hornchurch UDC was authorised by the Minister of Health to compulsory purchase 55.34 acres of land on the Elm Park estate.

The Council was able to build new houses gradually as they were granted loans from the Public Works Loan Commissioners, for example in February 1948 when the erection of 102 houses at Elm Park was given the green light. The minutes of the Hornchurch UDC Housing Committee, on 7th October 1948 record:

Elm Park naming of streets:

> The following place names be assigned to the new streets in course of construction on the Elm Park Estate:- Aldingham, Bowness, Derwent, Furness, Langdale, Penrith, Silverdale.

Aldingham Court under construction for Hornchurch UDC

These roads, radiating out from Rosewood Avenue, were later to become known as the Lake District Estate. Ambleside Avenue, Coniston Way, Carnforth Gardens and Easedale Gardens formed the rest of this section.

Map showing the original names for Elm Park and the core early development of the estate. A number of the street names such as Timmins, Keswick and Orchard were subsequently changed

Throughout this period, Costain continued to request that land obtained through compulsory purchase by the Council be released to them. It is interesting to note the number of planning applications in this period for the erection of sheds and garages by Elm Park residents.

In 1956 Elm Park Developments Co. Ltd. submitted for approval their scheme to name streets in the South Hornchurch area after officers and airmen who served at RAF Hornchurch. These roads leading off Mungo Park Road include Freeborne Gardens, Lovell Walk, Gray Gardens, Stephen Avenue and Adnams Walk.

By 1964, Hornchurch Urban District Council had provided 1,146 council house dwellings in Elm Park, the biggest concentration in the district.

Malan Square

Land at the corner of Elm Park Avenue and Rainham Road where Costain had extracted gravel for their house building was filled in and the Glens Estate of town houses was erected.

Elm Park Avenue leading to Upper Rainham Road before the Glens Estate was built

Airfield estate shops in the 1980s

The sale of RAF Hornchurch in 1963 soon led to further house building. The Airfield Estate took its street names from famous airfields such as Duxford and Northolt and a new shopping precinct was included in the development. Some of the airfield buildings remain. The Officers Mess is a medical centre and housing provided for the airmen and their families had been turned over to general use before the airfield was sold. Hoveringhams purchased much of the old airfield to extract sand and gravel before releasing it for further building or to Hornchurch Country Park which was created from 1980 on the site of the old airfield. The Suttons Farm Estate was built to the east of Rosebank Avenue. At the end of the 1980s small developments off Airfield Way were named from a list of pilots supplied by Ted Exall.

The Officer's Mess at RAF Hornchurch is now a medical centre. Other RAF Hornchurch quarters were handed over for civilian housing.

By Direction of The Secretary of State for Air

R.A.F. STATION
HORNCHURCH

London 18 miles   Dagenham 4 miles   Kent *via* Purfleet Tunnel 7 miles   Harwich 60 miles

TECHNICAL SITE, OFFICERS' MESS, LAND
Three Hangars and Numerous Substantial Brick Buildings

totalling over   **sq. 300,000 ft.**   net floor area

SUITABLE FOR A VARIETY OF PURPOSES
(Subject to Planning Permission)

THE FREEHOLD FOR SALE WITH VACANT POSSESSION

to be offered for sale on the Site by Public Auction by

KEMSLEYS
Chartered Surveyors and Auctioneers

WEDNESDAY, 27th FEBRUARY, 1963, at 3.30 p.m.

Auctioneers' Offices:
10 Western Road, Romford, Essex. *Telephone:* Romford 44175 (3 lines)
69 Old Broad Street, London, E.C.2

Left: Sale Catalogue RAF Hornchurch 1963

Above: Hoveringham's gravel extraction in the sixties

Below: Road names off Airfield Way

DOWDING WAY
LEADING TO
PEASE CLOSE
LEATHART CLOSE
ROBINSON CLOSE

ELM PARK CHURCHES AND OTHER PLACES OF WORSHIP

Historically, Elm Park was part of the Parish of Hornchurch and life in the locality was heavily influenced by the Church and the owners of the parish, New College, Oxford. Into the 19th century the parish church for the whole Liberty of Havering was the church of St Andrew in Hornchurch. Though there had been a chapel at Havering-atte-Bower at least since the 12th century it didn't establish a separation from Hornchurch until 1781 and even this was disputed by Hornchurch 20 years later. A chapel at Romford was first mentioned in 1177, but despite protests about payments to Hornchurch and the building of St Edward the Confessor with a burial ground in 1410, was still part of the Hornchurch Parish until 1849.

There was no Catholic Church in the Liberty of Havering until 1856, when the Church of St Edward was built in Romford, by Lord Petre. However, there were Recusants locally and in the eighteenth century Robert Prujean of Suttons Gate in Hornchurch converted to Catholicism, though he left later for a monastery in Flanders.

There were Non Conformists in Hornchurch and Romford from the 17th century. Elm Park provided the first synagogue in Hornchurch and other faiths such as Islam have only established premises elsewhere in the London Borough of Havering in more recent years.

PARISH CHURCH OF ST NICHOLAS, ELM PARK

Brian Cornwell has written this history of the Church of St Nicholas:

Once the parishes of Havering and of Romford were created, the Hornchurch Parish still extended north-west to Harold Wood, between the Rivers Beam and Ingrebourne and South to the Thames. As the population grew south of Hornchurch village the Church of St Andrew endeavoured to provide services for the parishioners there. In 1864 a small schoolroom was erected on New College land in South End Road opposite Wood Lane. This school was closed in 1899, but the building also served as a Chapel of Ease to St. Andrew's, Hornchurch, serving the scattered farms of the South Hornchurch area.

When work began on the Elm Park estate in 1934, St Andrew's recognised the urgent need for a new church to serve the rapidly expanding part of their parish, so a temporary dual-purpose building was built on a large plot of land bounded by Woodcote Avenue, Eyhurst Avenue and Timmins Avenue (now St Nicholas Avenue). The building was erected on the south-east corner of the site.

The old South End Road Chapel near Wood Lane c 1954

Interior of the original St Nicholas Church *courtesy Brian Cornwell*

The new church was dedicated to St Nicholas by the Rt. Rev. Henry Wilson, Bishop of Chelmsford on June 8th 1936. The *Essex Times* reported that so many people attended the dedication service that they could not all gain admission, and that the Vicar of Hornchurch, the Rev. C.K. Waller asked all members of the mother church to give up their seats so that Elm Park residents could find accommodation. The bishop gave the address and the service was attended by other clergy and the St Andrew's Churchwardens Messrs. R.W. Beard J.P. and F.G. Wright.

The Rev. H.G. King, a curate of St. Andrew's, became the first priest in charge of the new church. The church had a raised area at the west end for the choir. There was a folding partition to block off the sanctuary and a small tower south of the sanctuary with a priest's vestry and choir vestry above. Heating was provided by two coke stoves. In 1937 a wooden hall was built, paid for by R.W. Beard J.P., providing space for the branches of the uniformed organisations and various other church groups to meet; leaving the church solely for worship.

In 1939 a Conventional District of St. Nicholas Elm Park with South Hornchurch was formed with the Rev. G. Griffith Thomas as its first Priest-in-Charge. Most of the early Elm Park parishioners came from parts of East London where High Church traditions were more usual than at Hornchurch. Once Elm Park was freed from Hornchurch there was a move to the High Church and vestments were used for the first time in 1939. Following the outbreak of war in September 1939 the Rev. Thomas became a Chaplain to the Forces, in 1941.

Ecumenical Good Friday procession through Elm Park. The Baptist Church banner is visible near the back of the procession. This shared service has been revived in more recent times. *courtesy Brian Cornwell*

Between 1941 and 1944 the Rev. A. Harvey Webb was temporary Priest-in-Charge. In 1944 Canon Courthorpe, Vicar of Hornchurch, took temporary charge of the Conventional District. Unfortunately the absence of housing for the priest saw the temporary Priest in Charge of 1945, the Rev T.G.R. Hughes, resign following the resignation of the Rev. G. Griffith Thomas who came out of the forces but could not find a house.

The appointment of Rev. S.S. Adkins as Priest-in-Charge in 1946 was important in addressing a major problem in the new Conventional District caused by the RAF closing the South End Road in 1941. The RAF erected a barrier, which made the old South Hornchurch chapel inaccessible to anyone other than RAF personnel.

The chapel closed in 1941 and was eventually demolished in 1955. In 1939 the Strong Memorial Hall was erected on the site of the present St John's Church in South Hornchurch. This had established full church organisations but was destroyed by enemy action in April 1941. The sizeable South Hornchurch population in the new Conventional District could only be reached from Elm Park via the Rainham Road, a country road with fields either side. For the priest with only a bicycle for transport, the task of serving the whole district became impossible. The South End Road remained closed well after the War ended, despite the efforts of the Hornchurch UDC to have it reopened.

The Rev. Adkins was appalled at the size of the District, and the fact that St Nicholas was the only Church of England building in use, with the furthest parts of the area being 3 miles away. He reported to the Bishop of Chelmsford.

Stone laying ceremony at St Nicholas Church October 9th 1955 *courtesy Brian Cornwell*

In 1949 a temporary hut, dedicated to St. John, was erected on the site of the Strong Memorial Hall to once again serve South Hornchurch parishioners. In 1950 the Rev Adkins was taken ill and resigned and the third Priest in Charge of Elm Park with South Hornchurch was appointed; the Rev. R.C. Jones.

In 1953 The Bishop of Barking attended a meeting at St Nicholas to explain proposals for a reorganisation of the district. St John's was transferred to the Rainham Parish of St Helen and St Giles. In 1955, work commenced on a new, St Nicholas Church.

The new church, built south of the existing one, was part funded by the sale of land for housing to the west of the church. The Foundation Stone was laid by Ald. Sir Frank Foster C.B.E. J.P., Chairman of the Essex County Council on October 9th 1955. On June 5th 1956, the new Church of St Nicholas was consecrated by the Bishop of Chelmsford, and in 1957 a new Vicarage was built to the north of the Church and Elm Park became a separate Parish. The Rev. R.C. Jones, who had been Priest-in-Charge for seven years, was then instituted as the first Vicar of Elm Park.

The architect of the church, J.J. Crowe, was responsible for some of the pre-war churches in the Havering. The church is an excellent building, built to a traditional plan and design. It includes a Chancel and Sanctuary to the east end and a Baptistry at the west end. The Lady (or South) Chapel is partly under a Bell Tower. There are North and South aisles as well as a North Chapel.

The stained glass east window is by Randall, and his signature of a lizard can be seen at the bottom of the window. The theme of the window is Christ seated on a rainbow throne, a theme common in old windows and paintings. The window is a joint memorial to a former Churchwarden, Mr W. Gillison, and Mr Ernest Whybrew, the driver killed in the train derailment at Elm Park on March 29th 1965.

Also in the south aisle there is a board recording the names of previous Vicars. The board is a memorial to the Rev. H.G. King, the first Priest-in-Charge in 1936.

1956-1968	Rev R.C. Jones
1969-1976	Rev J.M. Wells M.A.
1976-1980	Rev D.G. Woolfenden
1980-1993	Rev D.S. Miller
1994-1999	Rev R. Lloyd
2001	Rev R. Finch

When St. John's, South Hornchurch was transferred to Rainham there was a revision of the parish boundary. This had been in an inconvenient position, since when the Mungo Park Estate was built, the boundary ran through the middle of it.

Further revision in 1976 resulted in it running down the centre of Wood Lane. I was involved in a slight later revision regarding the Morecambe Close area, so that all the original Elm Park houses and the old South Hornchurch Chapel site are now included within the Elm Park Parish.

In 1994 the original church building and the Adking Hall were demolished and the new Church Centre built. New flats were built on the old church site, the Vicarage was sold too and 17, St Nicholas Avenue was purchased to be the new Vicarage.

On January 19th 2000 there was a serious fire at the Church, which destroyed most of the roof. Because the Church was left open to the elements for several months, further damage was done. A major restoration took place, and during this period services took place in the Church centre. The Licensing Service for the Rev. Richard Finch took place in the Assembly Hall, with the final part of the service taking place in the ruined

The old and the new St Nicholas Church together *courtesy Brian Cornwell*

Elm Park St Nicholas Church fire 2000

Church. The Church was re-dedicated and brought back into use by the Bishop of Chelmsford on 2nd June 2001. Rev. Finch was inducted as Vicar at this service. A memorial tablet in the south aisle commemorates the Millennium and the re-dedication after the fire.

Interesting though history and architecture may be, the purpose of the Parish Church is as a place of worship for the people who live within the Parish. So it is that from the day that the church opened in June 1939 until the present date, two or three services have taken place every Sunday and a mid-week service of Holy Communion. Other occasional services take place from time to time as well as baptisms, weddings and funerals. Many other groups and organisations meet in the church every week and always have done. Thousands of Elm Park residents have had some kind of contact with their Church here over all these years. Long may it be so.

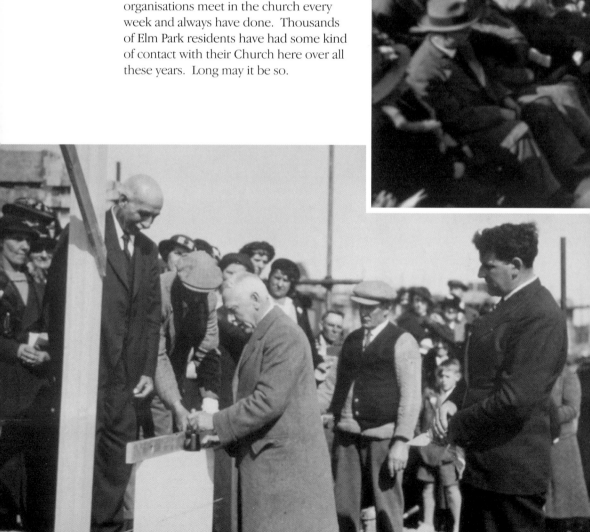

Stone laying ceremony at Elm Park Baptist church in 1938 *courtesy Brian Cornwell*

ELM PARK BAPTIST CHURCH

Elm Park Baptist church in Rosewood Avenue, originated in 1937 through
the work of the Rev William White. Sunday school began in one home and
Bible classes were held in another. Evening services were conducted in a dairy
distribution centre which was the only meeting space available. In 1938 a Sunday
school hall was opened and in February 1939 the church was formed with Mr B.U.
Sharpe as Lay Superintendent.

In 1940 the church closed for four months due to bomb damage. A Youth Hall
was opened in 1946 and a Manse was bought in 1946 as attempts to obtain
housing from Hornchurch Urban District Council were unsuccessful. The first
Baptist minister at Elm Park was Rev A.G. Hughes between 1948 and 1954. The
Rev. Leslie H. Moxham B.D. was minister between 1956 and 1960 and began plans
for the building of a new church. In 1962 a church building fund was inaugurated

with £2,000 and during the year a further £3,000 was collected through weekly donations and interest free loans from members of the congregation. In 1963, as part of their 25th anniversary celebrations, the new Elm Park Baptist Church was opened by the Rev W. Charles Johnson, secretary of the London Baptist Association. The church was dedicated by the Rev. M. Powell minister of Upminster Baptist Church and President of the Essex Baptist Association. Guests at the dedication ceremony included the Rev Hughes.

Sadly, in February 2006, an arson attack severely damaged the church. There were fears the building wouldn't survive and the congregation had to return to its roots, meeting in people's homes. The strong sense of ecumenical support, typical of Elm Park's history, was also evident as the Catholic Church made their hall available for the Baptists to conduct Sunday services. Another positive side effect was that Ardleigh Green Baptist Church, which had been earmarked for closure, was reopened for the Elm Park congregation and for local community use as a Family Centre. Thankfully Elm Park Baptist Church has been rebuilt and reopened again in 2008. A new stained glass window marked the revival of the church.

THE BRETHREN

The Brethren had a meeting place at Bethany Hall in Abbs Cross Lane which was registered in 1935. The building was demolished around 2003 and housing erected on the site, in what is now Bethany Close.

ELM PARK METHODIST CHURCH

Elm Park Methodist church in Freeborne Gardens off Mungo Park Road, was opened in 1957, in the Romford circuit. The original church building was demolished some years ago and flats were erected on the site with a new Methodist Church occupying the top floor.

ST ALBAN'S ROMAN CATHOLIC CHURCH

*This history of the origins of St Alban's Church was written by **Fr Stewart Foster, Diocesan Archivist and Historian of Brentwood Diocese** and first appeared in the February 2003 issue of **Brentwood News:***

The Comboni Missionaries (Verona Fathers) approached Bishop Doubleday (of the Brentwood Diocese) in 1937 to open a house of studies in Chigwell. This never materialised and the college opened instead in 1938 at Sunningdale, Berkshire.

In 1948, the Verona Fathers again approached Bishop Doubleday and his Coadjutor Bishop Beck, this time offering to take charge of a parish. In the winter of 1948—49, they were given responsibility for the Elm Park section of the Hornchurch parish. St Alban's church hall in Carnforth Gardens had been opened in 1939 (*on 3rd September the day war broke out*) by Monsignor Van Meenan and served as a Mass centre and annexe to St Mary's Primary School.

The first Verona Fathers, under Father John Cotta, lived at 45 Coronation Drive, and the parish of Elm Park was formally established in 1951 with Father Eric Grace as parish priest. The following year, the priests moved to 27 Coniston Way and in 1956 Father Hugh Toninello began his 35 year ministry as parish priest, ably assisted by other Verona Fathers, notably Father Polato, an accomplished musician.

Architects Burles Newton drew up a plan for a new church (inspired by the Church of St Zeno, Verona), which was constructed at a cost of £33,000 on a new site between Langdale Gardens and Ullswater Way. Bishop Wall opened the church of St Alban on 14 June 1960. A parish centre was opened in 1969. Bishop Casey consecrated St Alban's church on 31 January 1978. A new presbytery, next door to the church was also built. In 1991, after 42 years service, the Verona Fathers relinquished pastoral care of the parish to the Diocese of Brentwood.

Artists impression of St Alban's RC Church as planned in 1963.

ELM PARK AFFILIATED SYNAGOGUE

Opening of the Elm Park Synagogue September 1949

The synagogue in Elm Park was established in 1939 and became affiliated to the United Synagogue in 1948. At this time there were 48 male seat holders and in 1949 a permanent building was erected in Woburn Avenue, next to the railway line. The synagogue was opened on Sunday 18th September 1949 by Miss Shirley Tabor, daughter of the President. She was taking the place of her mother who had died shortly before. Commemoration windows to the late Mrs Tabor were also unveiled. Councillor W. J. Bush, Chairman of Hornchurch Urban District Council, was presented with a book of Jewish thoughts by the Very Rev. Chief Rabbi, Israel Brodie. The service was conducted by the Rev. I. Miller assisted by the choir of the Great Synagogue. Synagogue membership grew in the 1950s and there were 87 male seat holders in 1960. By 1985 there were only 37 members of the Elm Park Synagogue and by 1999 it had been demolished and plans were submitted for houses to be built on the site. Memorials and other artefacts from the synagogue were transferred to the Romford Synagogue.

OTHER CHRISTIAN CHURCHES

In the 1950s the Assembly Hall was used by the Church of Jesus Christ of Latter Day Saints (Mormons). A number of new churches have arrived in Elm Park in recent years. These include Arise Metropolitan Assembly convened by Apostle George Akalonu and Christ Life Church led by Pastor Ola Fasanmiwhich both in Elm Park Assembly Hall; and Eagles Christian Connections which has held meetings above the Co-op in Elm Park Avenue.

The Synagogue after closure in 1999. *Courtesy Frank Harris, Benjamin Tobin, Tymsyder Publishing*

Synagogue interior photographed after closure 1999 *Courtesy Frank Harris, Benjamin Tobin, Tymsyder Publishing*

ELM PARK SCHOOLS

Education for most children in the Elm Park district originated with **SIBELL SKEALE'S INFANTS SCHOOL**, South End Road, South Hornchurch. The school was funded from the Skeale's Charity. This school began in the church mission hall in the South End Road and taught children to the age of eight and in 1871 there were 63 pupils. From 1885 the school received an annual government grant. In 1890 it was taken over by the local school board and in 1899 South Hornchurch Board School replaced it.

Eileen Wilson remembers Miss Skeale's School House:

> Along the South End Road near the junction of Wood Lane, there was an old school house with a sign above the door declaring it to be 'Miss Skeale's School House'. The bell that was situated on the roof has been kept in the community as a memento. It used to conjure up for me visions of children using slates and chalk as writing materials and little girls with pinafores sitting at their desks. On reflection, I don't think the building was bigger than our garden shed and I do wonder how many children were taught there at any one time.

ABBS CROSS SCHOOL and ARTS COLLEGE

Abbs Cross School opened in 1958 as a Technical High School that was attended by both boys and girls. The name came from the school's location in Abbs Cross Lane. This was once Apsi Cross and is said to be associated with William le Aps, mentioned in 1233 in Hornchurch Priory documents. He is believed to have lived in Hornchurch near the High Street. Another theory is that the name came from Saint Ebba, the name being corrupted to Saint Abbs.

Abbs Cross School 1959

In 1973 the school became a comprehensive and in 1974 an additional building was added to cope with demand. What were once farm fields are now extensive playing fields with pitches for rugby, soccer, netball, a cricket square and hard tennis courts. The school now boasts a three million pounds sports and leisure centre that includes a sports hall, swimming pool and fitness centre. Facilities are also open to the community.

ALBANY SCHOOL

P.E. lesson at Maylands County Secondary Modern girls school shortly after opening in 1962.

Originally known as Maylands School, Broadstone Road, it opened in 1962 as a Secondary Modern School for girls. In 1982 it became co-educational and was renamed Albany School. The Albany now has business and enterprise specialist status.

AYLOFF PRIMARY SCHOOL
History of Ayloff School taken from the 50 years celebration brochure 1988:

Ayloff School

Ayloff School opened in April 1938 after pressure was brought to bear on the local education authorities by Elm Park parents. Promised five schools in Costain's advertising brochures, the original schools of Suttons and the recently opened Benhurst Primary School could not cope with the numbers of school aged children moving into the area.

Letter from local resident dated September 1937:

Dear Sir

    ...I wish to point out the deplorable state of affairs as regards the schools on this estate... This I suddenly realised when my own son became of school age and we tried to get him in what school there is on this estate. He was taken for the first time on Monday morning and enrolled and was kept there for a day. But on the Tuesday morning we were informed that there was no room for him there and he would have to go to the Assembly Hall. Now I strongly object to this, not only from the health point of view, as it is not fit for children being very draughty, but, as a member of the Residents Association, I have been keeping the Hall open as a place of amusement not education, which, I was under the impression was covered by the local rates, yours....

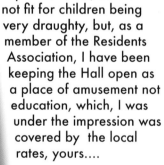

1958 pupils at Ayloff School celebrate their 100% attendance over 4 weeks. Richard and Alan Poulain and Michael and Wendy Hynsen are pictured.

AWARDED TO THIS CLASS FOR BEST ATTENDANCE LAST WEEK

The school name was taken from the eminent local family of Ayloffe who lived at the manor house of Bretons and whose tomb can be seen in St. Andrew's Parish Church, Hornchurch.

The school opened with places for 450 children and on the first day the older children had to carry their desks from the Assembly Hall round to Ayloff School. The school was closed on 3rd September 1939 at the outbreak of war. Older children had some education by correspondence courses and home tuition centres were set up for the younger children. Education at the

Aerial view of Ayloff School in the nineties

school was spasmodic over the following year often depending on the state of the trenches where children hid during air raids. On Saturday August 31st 1940 during the Battle of Britain the school suffered two direct hits on the trench near the railway line and the school was finally closed a week later. Amazingly little damage occurred to the buildings and the school finally reopened on January 6th 1942.

Numbers of children at the school continued to rise, reaching a peak in the mid 1950's with numbers ranging from 800-900. Each class could have between 36 to 53 children. Now, due to falling rolls, the school is about to move to an alternative location whilst a new school is built on the site to accommodate children from Ayloff and Dunningford Schools. The new school will be known as The Elm Park Primary School.

BENHURST PRIMARY SCHOOL

Benhurst School was opened in 1936 with temporary buildings and takes its name from the road in which it stands. The name broken down into its component parts translates as **Ben** a "mountain peak" and **Hurst** "a wood" The buildings erected in 1936 still serve the school today but with several important alterations. The majority of these took place from the late 1980's to 2009. These include a school library, new dining hall, IT suite, toilets, office area and sick bay. Since 1936 there have only been four head teachers at the school and the current headmaster, Ian Trafford, has been there over 20 years.

Rod Moffatt remembers his time at Benhurst School with affection:

I started school at five years old and for the first few weeks did only half days, the mothers coming to collect the young ones at lunch time. After the first year I was allowed to go to and from school alone as I lived close by in Warren Drive. The teachers I remember were all ladies except for Mr Tew the headmaster. He was the first head and was still there in 1957 when my son went to the school. I do not remember any other men there, perhaps because they had all joined the forces. The school day started when the bell was rung in the playground and you all had to line up, one behind the other, in front of the teachers. Then you marched into school for assembly in the hall, where prayers were said and Mr Tew read out the notices.

Everyone had a third of a pint bottle of milk at break time and the very youngest children had to have an afternoon sleep on little mattresses on the floor. You always had to stand when a teacher or the head came into the classroom. Most lessons were by rote, ink had to be mixed every day by the ink monitor, which was very messy! You sat in two seater desks all facing the front and chairs had to be put on top of the desks at home time. The only punishment I remember having was to stand in the corner of the class, probably for talking during lessons or not doing my homework. The classrooms had hot water pipes running round the walls, no radiators, and on cold days we all used to sit on them and try to warm our hands and legs, which were bare then, as short trousers were worn by all the boys. The lucky ones were those whose desks were next to those pipes.

During the War some classes were held in people's homes. But while we were at school, if the siren sounded we had to march into the shelters, which were along side the fences of the back gardens in Warren Drive and all the teachers got us all singing or reciting our tables to try and take our minds off what was happening outside. In the playground you showed off your latest finds of war bits and pieces. I know mine was taking the tail fin of the fire bomb that had come through our roof at home! There

Children in the playground of Benhurst School – note the uncovered toilet block in the foreground.

Benhurst School 1937

were always plenty of bits of shrapnel, shell fragments and spent bullets to show off.

Towards the end of 1944 came the 11 plus exams, which we had to take at Drury Falls School, Upminster Bridge. I remember well the apprehension as I caught the train from Elm Park station and I failed!

After the War there was a very good Youth Club set up after school at Benhurst. I can remember joining the class that was using the "new" plastic to make things for the house like table lamps, butter dishes and toast racks! If the plastic had to be bent it was done with a heated former and if two pieces needed to be fixed together you used ether, which was kept under lock and key by the teacher. Very wise as it was easy to be overcome by it! There was also entertainment in the hall with a wind up gramophone and a piano.

Benhurst School football team. District Champions 1953-54

Brittons Secondary School shortly after it opened in 1952

BRITTONS SCHOOL

Brittons School, situated in South Hornchurch, was opened in 1952 as a mixed secondary modern school. It was enlarged in 1964. Now known as Brittons School and Technology College it has just over 1,000 pupils. Also on the site is a pre-school group for two to four year olds called Brittons Babes, adult education classes are held there, and an army cadet group meets there regularly.

Terry Malby recalls his school days:

> I was part of the first year intake at Dunningfords. I remember thinking how modern and exciting the school seemed. I was probably one of the naughtiest boys there as I was always getting told off.
>
> After that, I went to Brittons. I'll never forget my first day. There was a big banister along the stairway and I just couldn't resist the temptation to slide down it. The headmaster caught me and I got caned as punishment. The cane was used freely in those days – it might not have stopped me being naughty but I never committed the same antic twice. I'd sometimes play truant and walk to Romford market. There were cattle, sheep and goats in the market then; much more exciting than going to lessons!

DUNNINGFORD PRIMARY SCHOOL

Dunningford School opened in January 1955, as separate Infant and Junior Schools, to cope with the huge number of children needing primary school education in the Elm Park area. The Reception Class consisted of 46 children! A year later the school roll stood at a combined total of 567 children. Most of the children had transferred from the overcrowded Ayloff School. The name Dunningford had been taken from the farm of the same name that had previously occupied the land on which the school was built. School dinners were started in February 1955, but were sent over from Ayloff School. There were some initial teething problems with boilers and flooding pipes in the toilets but, by the November half term, the new black and red school uniform had been issued.

In the mid 1960's Dunningford School undertook the unusual step of teaching a disabled thalidomide boy alongside able bodied classmates. A logbook entry notes 'wonderful reaction from the children as D joined them in the playground' and a couple of weeks later 'Dr. Gorman was astonished at the progress he had made and the way the children reacted'.

1958/59 netball team at Dunningford School

Dunningford School cap badge.

In 1985 the infants and junior schools amalgamated and more recently have shared their premises with other agencies including First Step Opportunities Play Group and the Bridge Nursery, thus continuing that earlier commitment of supporting the education of disadvantaged children. Unfortunately, due to falling rolls, the school closed in July 2009 after over 50 years of serving local children and the wider community.

Del Ramsey recalls his days at Dunningford:

> I went to Dunningford from 1958. I could walk from my home in St Andrews Avenue. I remember having free school milk – it was delicious in winter, when it stood in crates outside but not so nice in the summer, when the hot weather made it turn very quickly. We were also given black malt to drink which was dreadful!

R J MITCHELL PRIMARY SCHOOL

Mitchell Junior School was opened in 1967 and a separate infant school opened four years later. The school is built on the parade ground of the former RAF Hornchurch and its first pupils were from RAF families living in the married quarters on the opposite side of the South End Road. The school had been built in advance of the houses of the Airfield Estate which were intended to be its primary intake. The school is named after Reginald Joseph Mitchell who designed the Spitfire aircraft, which was used to great effect by the pilots of Hornchurch during the Battle of Britain. Unfortunately Mitchell did not live to see the success of the Spitfire as a fighter plane, as he died in 1937 aged just 42. The school was opened by Air Vice Marshall Jones and Air Commodore Alan Deere who presented the school with a replica RAF Hornchurch badge.

Architect's model of Mitchell Infants School

Air Vice Marshall R.I. Jones and the Havering Mayor, Alderman W.A. Sibley at the official opening of Mitchell School 2nd December 1968.

In July 1983 a memorial stone to commemorate those who served at the aerodrome was unveiled by Air Marshall Sir Harry Broadhurst who was the commanding officer at Hornchurch in 1940. The four school teams are named after fighter pilots Broadhurst, Deere, Stephen, and Tuck who flew from RAF Hornchurch during the Battle of Britain and their portraits hang in the school hall. The school tie is an RAF tie and R.J. Mitchell is one of only two schools in the United Kingdom allowed to wear one as part of their school uniform.

SANDERS DRAPERS SCHOOL

The head Mr Lovett with the teaching staff at Suttons Senior Boys School after the war.

The school, originally named Suttons Senior School, was opened in 1938 by Lady Simon with separate girls and boys departments. Although they shared the same site the children were strictly forbidden to mix during school hours. At the outbreak of War the school was closed so that air-raid shelters could be built. The school opened and closed several times because of the danger of enemy action and when the Battle of Britain started the children spent many hours in the shelters. In 1943 the school was saved by the gallant action of Raimond Sanders Draper, who stayed in his aircraft rather than bail out, in order to avoid crashing into the school. He was killed instantly and was only 25 years old. In 1973, when the school became a comprehensive, the name

was changed to Sanders Draper to honour the selfless pilot. The school has maintained association with his family and some years ago his daughter Anne visited the school. Each year the school proudly celebrates Sanders Draper Day so that young people continue to have an understanding of the school's history and the values that it represents.

ST ALBAN'S CATHOLIC PRIMARY SCHOOL

For many years there was no Catholic primary school in Elm Park and children had to attend St. Mary's Hornchurch, La Salette Rainham or even St. Ursula's Harold Hill. Some infant classes from St. Mary's were accommodated in the church hall, Carnforth Gardens. A permanent Catholic school in Elm Park had been planned since 1962 but was not completed until 1971. Bishop Casey officially opened the school on 21 June 1973. The school is named after the parent church of St. Alban's in Elm Park. St. Alban is venerated as the first English martyr and the school badge represents his martyr's crown with ears of wheat to symbolise holy mass.

SCOTTS PRIMARY SCHOOL

The school takes its name from Scott's Farm, which was situated off the South End Road close to Albyn's Farm, which now forms part of the Hornchurch Country Park. The school badge features a farm gate and two ears of corn to commemorate the farm and the wings of the RAF and a flight path representing the airfield. This serves as a reminder that the school is built on land that was previously part of RAF Hornchurch.

ELM PARK LIBRARY

When the estate opened in 1935 there were no plans for a library, as readers were expected to use the one in Harrow Lodge Park. By 1938 Essex County Council had purchased a site for a new library at the intersection of Maybank Avenue and the South End Road, where Carrie's Hall stands today.

But the outbreak of the Second World War stopped development plans and as a wartime expedient the St. Nicholas Church Hall Juvenile Centre was opened with a stock of about three hundred books. This was open for one hour a week on Friday afternoons and about eighty children used the service. In 1947 the County Council resumed discussions concerning a library building for Elm Park and proposed a temporary building on the site already purchased. As a result of post war austerity in Britain, many public buildings such as school classrooms and libraries were in the form of temporary 'huts'. Now began nearly a decade of negotiations between the Essex County Council Libraries Committee and the Hornchurch Urban District Council.

For some years the favoured plan was place a small library in the Assembly Hall annexe or somewhere on the surrounding land. Then in 1954 it was suggested that an entirely new site be bought in The Broadway, an idea finally abandoned in 1957 when the site owners decided to build shops instead. It was during this same period that, in response to local demand, Elm Park became a weekly stop on the Mobile Library's route. The matter was finally resolved when the Buildings and Supply Committee of Essex County Council decided in May 1955 to erect a temporary building on the present site. The library was officially opened on 5th October 1956 to great enthusiasm from readers young and old.

Elm Park Library shortly after it opened in 1956

The premises served the local community for over fifty years until it reached the end of its economic life. In June 2008 the bulldozers moved in and quickly demolished the building and on April 27th 2009 a brand new library opened its doors. The Mayor of Havering, Cllr Roger Ramsey, officially opened the library at a ceremony on Monday 8th June 2009.

The roof is fitted with solar panels, the sedum roof improves insulation, absorbs some CO2 and other pollutants and provides wildlife habitat. The library was the winner in 2008 Havering Business Awards for Sustainable Design and Construction due to its low carbon footprint. But what is important to local users is that their library is back again at the hub of the community.

Demolition of Elm Park Library 2008

New Elm Park Library interior 2009

ELM PARK HOTEL

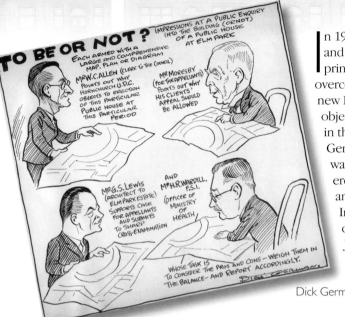

In 1935, Costain became a public company and the strict Methodist teetotaller principles of the Chairman were overcome to provide a public house in the new Elm Park development plans. Local objections to a public house are captured in this wonderful cartoon by Dick German. By May 1937 an application was granted by Hornchurch UDC to erect and license the Elm Park Hotel and in July 1938 it opened its doors. In the seventies the pub hosted star comedians such as Mike Reid and Jimmy Jones and was a popular venue for live band performances.

Dick German cartoon about the public inquiry into the building of a public house in Elm Park.

Elm Park Hotel 1934 plans by Samuel Yeo

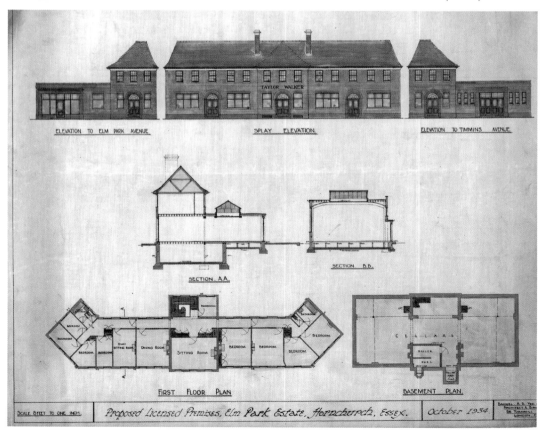

THE RAILWAY YEARS

There has been a railway running through the area that became Elm Park since 1885 when the London, Tilbury and Southend line was opened. In 1902, the Metropolitan District Railway ran a service along the section between Barking and Upminster, sharing the London, Tilbury and Southend tracks.

Work on the District Line began in 1865, with the first stations opened in 1868. These were: Paddington, Bayswater, Notting Hill Gate, Kensington, Gloucester Road and South Kensington. By the early 1900s, District Line trains were running to East Ham, although one train ran once every morning and again in the evening to Upminster, stopping at Dagenham en route.
In those days, a train from Upminster to Charing Cross took 54 minutes – only a minute longer than they did a century later!

Elm Park Station under construction c 1934

In 1923 railways were grouped into four companies and the Southend line became part of the London, Midland Scottish (LMS) Company.

In 1932, new tracks for the District Line were laid and new stations were built along the route from Barking to Upminster. Upney, Dagenham Heathway and Becontree were built in 1932 (Becontree used to be called Gale Street Halt until 1926).

Upminster Bridge was built in 1934 and Elm Park was opened in 1935. What is now Dagenham East station was once known as Dagenham, until 1st May 1949.

Elm Park station was officially opened on 13th May 1935 by Sir Hilton and Lady Young.

Elm Park Station 1937

Station platform 1935

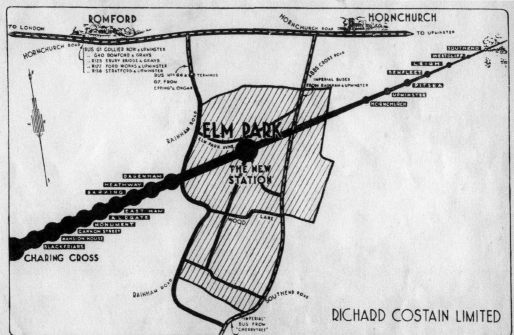

THE LINE TO THE NEW HOME CENTRE

East or West, wherever your work lies or your friends live, ELM PARK Station will offer you quick, cheap and frequent trains to get there and back in comfort. The map above shows the line to live on and the centre to live in.

Costain show how well connected Elm Park is to the rail network.

The LMS seaside special to Southend steams through Elm Park, late forties. The newly built Elm Park Synagogue is visible on the right.

Station platform late forties

The station buildings on this section of the District Line were similar in design and typical of the 1930s period. A noteworthy feature is the 700ft island platform canopy, which was the first type of this welded construction to be used in Britain. Some say this was the first British Weld Record!

Unsurprisingly, the numbers of rail users grew and in 1936, Elm Park was awarded the LMS Shield for having the biggest passenger increase across the London Midland region. Even today, Elm Park enjoys the highest footfall of the District Line section between Barking and Upminster.

In 1936 there was a ruling by the District Line operators which created some uproar. In those days, there were first class facilities: bizarrely, non First Class carriages were denoted as Third Class. The ruling stated that:

> **"If Third Class carriages are full, passengers with Third Class Tickets are allowed to sit in the First Class Carriage, providing they are east of Charing Cross. West of Charing Cross, they are permitted to stand in First Class but not sit."**

By 1939, railway tickets were being issued to commuters on a Sunday to alleviate the long queues on a Monday morning. Tube users today might say that not much has changed over 70 years.

ELM PARK STATION

ROMFORD · *The New* HOME CENTRE · ESSEX

ON YOUR DOORSTEP

CHEAP, DIRECT TRAVEL TO TOWN & SEA

ELM PARK TO	Cheap Day Return.	ORDINARY.		SEASONS.		
		Single.	Return.	Weekly.	Monthly.	Quarterly.
	s. d.	s. d.	s. d.	s. d.	£ s. d.	£ s. d.
Dagenham	3	2½	5	—	7 6	1 0 0
Heathway	4	4	8	2 5	9 6	1 5 9
Becontree... ...	4	4	8	3 0	11 9	1 11 9
Upney	6	6	1 0	3 5	13 6	1 16 9
Barking	6	6	1 0	3 9	15 0	2 0 9
East Ham	8	7½	1 3	4 4	17 3	2 6 6
Upton Park ...	9	9	1 6	4 9	18 9	2 11 3
Plaistow	9	9	1 6	5 2	1 0 6	2 15 9
West Ham	9	9	1 6	—	1 1 0	2 17 3
Bromley	10	10	1 8	5 3	1 1 0	2 17 3
Bow Road... ...	—	11½	1 11	5 9	1 2 0	2 19 6
Mile End	—	1 1	2 2	5 9	1 2 0	2 19 6
Stepney Green ...	—	1 2	2 2	—	1 3 0	3 2 6
Whitechapel ...	—	1 4	2 5	6 6	1 3 0	3 2 6
St. Mary's	—	1 6	2 7	—	1 4 3	3 5 3
Aldgate East ...	—	1 8	2 9	—	1 6 0	3 10 6
Fenchurch St. or Mark Lane	1 8	1 8	2 11	6 6	1 6 0	3 10 6
Monument	—	1 8	2 11	—	1 8 3	3 17 6
Cannon Street ...	—	1 8	2 11	—	1 9 0	3 19 9
Mansion House ...	1 10	1 9	3 1	8 6	1 9 0	3 19 9
Blackfriars	—	1 9	3 1	8 9	1 12 0	4 7 6
Temple	—	1 9	3 3	—	1 13 6	4 11 0
Charing Cross ...	2 0	1 9	3 3	8 9	1 14 0	4 12 3

N.B.—The Cheap Day Returns operate daily by any train after 9.30 a.m., and on Sundays any train, return any train day of issue. Third-class fares only quoted.

Rail fares from Elm Park 1937

Following nationalisation in 1948, ownership of the station passed from London Midland and Scottish Railway to British Rail. Mainline services stopped serving intermediate stations in 1962. Ownership passed from British Rail to London Underground in 1969.

Christine White remembers the station in the 1950s:

> In 1956, it was not a heavily used station. I used to go to the platform and meet my father from work. A platform ticket cost one penny. A lady called Sarah Stock ran the kiosk inside the station. There was also a parcel collection point and a bicycle stand inside the station. Our home overlooked the station and we could see straight into the Ladies Waiting Room!

RAIL CRASH

Many residents who lived in Elm Park in the 1960s can remember the tragic train crash that occurred on 29th March 1965. It happened in the evening rush hour between Elm Park and Dagenham East and two people died. Residents in St Andrews Avenue can recall casualties being taken through their back gardens to awaiting ambulances. The train was derailed as a result of a concrete obstacle on the line. Nobody was prosecuted for this crime.

The train and underground network was a vital link for both commuters and social activities. Elm Park was built as a new town to accommodate people from the East End of London and provide them a fresh start in life. Many relied on the City of London and docks for employment.

Edna Bono remembers her daily commute:

> I used to travel to the Monument every day for work. Commuting was an enjoyable experience, as the same people used to occupy the same carriages and people got to know each other well. It was just like being part of a club.

Christine White was another commuter during the 1960s:

> I got to know the ticket collector quite well, as I would often fall asleep on the train from London and end up in Upminster. I was warned if I continued to do this, I would be charged the extra fare!

The trains that came to Elm Park also provided a wonderful link to Upminster, where families could treat themselves to a steam train journey to Southend.

Terry Malby has fond memories of such trips:

> Nothing surpassed the experience of hanging your head out of the window and being belted with steam and smut from the locomotive. To a young boy, full of adventure, this was seventh heaven.

ON THE BUSES –
THE ELM PARK WAY

In the early days of the development of the Elm Park estate, bus connections to the area were poor. But we shouldn't forget that before World War II, walking to Romford or Hornchurch was not considered to be a hardship and also that many people owned bicycles and cycling was the method of choice in getting from A to B. And not just locally either! It was not unusual for some dockworkers to cycle to their jobs in today's City Docklands.

In January 1939 the Romford Times' reported:

> 'Elm Park residents want an improved bus service from Laburnum Road (now that the Rainham Road is made up) to Elm Park Broadway, and a further improvement to all existing rail services'.

The Traffic Advisory Committee (Romford Division) responded:

> 'Residents can go to Upminster Bridge from Elm Park to catch a bus to Romford; or walk to Abbs Cross and catch an infrequent bus from Rainham to Romford; or walk the whole distance'!!!

However, by April 1939, the single decker 252A bus route was extended from Romford and Roneo Corner via Rainham Road to the Broadway at Elm Park.

Two of the Elm Park buses at their terminus in Rainham

Route 253 served Rainham from White Post Corner, to South End Road, Abbs Cross Lane, Roneo Corner and to the Parkside Hotel. As a concession, the bus route extended to Collier Row on Saturdays after 12.30pm and summer Sundays after 10.30am!

Between 1940 and 1958, the bus routes changed and the main buses serving Elm Park were the 123 and 165.

- **123 - South Hornchurch (South End Road), Elm Park, Roneo Corner, Collier Row, North Romford, Havering-Atte-Bower, Stapleford Abbotts, Passingford Bridge, Stanford Rivers, Ongar**
- **165 - Collier Row (Clockhouse Lane), Roneo Corner, Abbs Cross Lane, Elm Park, South Hornchurch, Rainham (White Post Corner)**

By 1962, the 252 route was developed to encompass Elm Park and provided a useful service to Romford and Collier Row. The 165 route also experienced a slightly altered journey but continued to serve the residents of Elm Park.

- **252 -** South Hornchurch (Wood Lane), Elm Park, Roneo Corner, Mawney Road, White Hart Lane, Collier Row Road, Lowshoe Lane
- **165 -** Havering Park (Hunters Grove), Collier Row, Roneo Corner, Abbs Cross Lane, Elm Park, Mungo Park Road, Cherry Tree Lane, Rainham War Memorial)
-

Apart from cosmetic changes to the routes over the next three decades, the 165 and 252 buses continued to serve communities between Elm Park, Collier Row and Romford. In 1992, the 365 route was introduced alongside the 252 and 165 routes, giving even more accessibility across the Borough of Havering. By 2008, the number of bus routes had increased to four, allowing people to connect further afield to the Lakeside Shopping Centre in Thurrock.

THE GREAT STORM OF 1987

Chris Hipperson recalls:

We were woken by the high winds at about 4am on Friday 16th October. I didn't realize how serious the situation was and kept trying to get back to sleep. The double glazing probably cut down a lot of the noise but we still heard glass tinkling and breaking in the greenhouse. I thought that the apples and pears were being blown off our trees and smashing the glass. (In the morning, when we got up, we discovered it wasn't our greenhouse that had suffered the damage but three belonging to various neighbours.) I wasn't frightened at all as it never occurred to me that there was any danger.

Our son Tom got up at 6am and got dressed to go out on his paper round and so we got up too. Looking out we at last realised how bad things were. I phoned 'Newsbox' to ask Pete if he expected the newspaper boys in? 'No' he said "it's too dangerous to send the boys out and besides no papers are here!'

At 7.30am Tom and I strolled along Warren Drive to survey the damage. Telephone wires were trailing, trees in front gardens were blown down and a huge lime tree lay across the road at the Abbs Cross end of Warren Drive. Many fences and walls were destroyed and leaves and rubbish were everywhere. Our own phone was only connected intermittently and branches from the lime tree outside our house were snapped off.

My husband drove me to work in Gidea Park and then on to Walthamstow. Luckily we took the Mini because several times we drove up on to the pavement to get round fallen trees, otherwise I don't think we'd have got through. That afternoon Tom and I walked round Elm Park taking photographs of the devastation and damage.

Havering Council later reported that 5,000 trees had been destroyed in the borough, tons of debris had been cleared from the streets, pavements had been torn up by falling trees, and there was widespread damage to roofing, fences and windows. Local school children stayed home and 50 schools sustained damage ranging from windows blown out to sections of roofing ripped off. The unpredicted high winds began at 3am and the Council had soon set up an emergency control centre at the Upper Rainham Road depot. Winds of 100 miles per hour were recorded in the Isle of Wight and along the south coast. In London winds of 94mph were recorded and in Havering winds gusting up to 100mph.

Many cars were destroyed by falling trees, walls and chimney stacks fell down, power lines were affected and street and domestic lighting failed, as well as telephones. Scores of plate glass windows and bus shelters shattered, advertising hoardings and scaffolding collapsed but incredibly, apart from one serious injury, only minor accidents were reported. Council workmen worked along side police and fire-fighters to clear roads whilst having to dodge flying tiles and other debris. Most roads were open to traffic by Friday evening. The District Line ran a restricted service during Friday and London bus services resumed in the afternoon with 60 percent of normal coverage. But it took many weeks to clean up the roads and repair all the damage to property.

Aftermath of the 1987 hurricane. The owner of the black cab didn't even hear the storm.

MODERN ELM PARK

The new Millennium brought other challenges. Two of the churches in Elm Park suffered serious fires and a Millennium tree planting ceremony at St Nicholas Church couldn't take place until 2001! However these hurdles have been overcome and proved the importance of the churches to the local community and the strong relationship between the individual churches.

Millennium tree planting ceremony 11th February 2001. Rev Richard Finch, Chris Hipperson and the Archdeacon of West Ham, the Venerable Michael Fox.

Elm Park has needed help from elsewhere to deal with some of the difficulties common in suburban areas around London.

In 2003, Elm Park was selected as a test site in London to have classical music played in the station, as a measure to combat anti social behaviour and calm crowds. This initiative was such a success that over 40 other London underground stations have now introduced the system.

Also in 2003, the London Development Agency provided funding of £250,000 to revitalise Elm Park. Residents wanted "to see progress – we want to see results" and a Steering Group was established to plan improvements over a three year period. The money was spent on townscape improvements, business assistance for shops and essential basic training earning opportunities for the unemployed. As a separate exercise, new street lighting was also installed in the town centre.

This attempt to renew the town was a start and inspired some residents to take things into their own hands.

Elm Park Regeneration Partnership

Ingrid Brandon explains

A small group of like-minded individuals in Elm Park believed that re-building civic pride in Elm Park was key in the regeneration of a community and that the local shops and businesses were instrumental in providing reasons for people to love the place where they live, work and shop. This motivated them to form the Elm Park Regeneration Partnership. Their mission was to build a prosperous and vibrant community "with small village feel but big town appeal".

In June 2005, they organised and launched the first Elm Park Fiesta: a day where the town centre and local amenity groups could showcase themselves and an occasion when visitors and residents could be introduced and reacquainted with the services on their doorstep.

With the Broadway closed to traffic, most of Elm Park centre became pedestrianised (probably for the first time in its history!) as shops brought their insides "outside". The library and local churches entered into the spirit of the day with exhibitions, competitions and sales and people began to see what makes Elm Park so special.

Encouraged by positive feedback, the Partnership organised another event before Christmas and persuaded the council to provide a Christmas tree and festive illuminations. The shops stayed open to offer Elm Park's first late night shopping occasion. This event was called "Illuminating Elm Park" a pun on words designed to emphasise the spotlight being put on the town centre. The organisers also encouraged shopkeepers to dress and light up their windows for the occasion. In the summer, bunting is put up across the Broadway for the Fiestas.

Elm Park Fiesta poster 2006

Elm Park Regeneration Partnership

Saturday 3 June
Elm Park Town Centre
12 – 4pm

Elm Park Fiesta 2006

SUPPORT YOUR LOCAL TOWN CENTRE

A fun-packed programme including:

Childrens' rides

Shopping discounts

Live entertainment

Beach themed competitions

Giveaways

Bargains

Historic Elm Park Exhibition

Local community displays

BRINGING YOU ALL THE FUN OF THE SEASIDE

Posters sponsored by Reeve, Fisher & Sands - Elm Park's Property Lawyers

For Elm Park's fifth Fiesta birthday celebrations, Eva Regan and Sadie Hunter took first prize in the fancy dress competition.

I ♥ ELM PARK

For the organisers, these were new concepts never before experienced in Elm Park, but history shows that similar ideas had already been introduced during Elm Park's Civic Week in 1939. There's nothing new under the sun .

As the estate nears its 75th birthday, buildings and organisations in Elm Park have been reaching their own historic milestones. The Elm Park Horticultural Guild celebrated 70 years in 2007 and at the same time St Nicholas Church marked 50 years of the new church building. Residents have an increased sense of Elm Park's history and identity and in 2009 the Elm Park Regeneration Partnership adopted a small piece of derelict land beside the station to display a gallery of images featuring "My Elm Park".

Like many other small shopping centres, Elm Park has had to compete with the large out- of- town retail malls, such as Lakeside in Thurrock and Bluewater in Kent; and more particularly, the supermarket chains. Despite this, Elm Park continues to offer an enviable range of independent shops, ranging from home furnishings and garden supplies to pet shops and electrical repairs. The Halifax Building Society, which was instrumental in providing mortgages for the buyers of the new homes in Elm Park remains; as does the Co-op grocery store on part of the premises once occupied by the Grays Co-operative. The former estate offices at the end of Coronation Drive are now appropriately occupied by a firm of property lawyers, Reeve, Fisher and Sands.

Comic Legend Sir Norman Wisdom paid a surprise social visit to his friends Rita and Ray Dempsey, owners of Another Nice Mess, in January 2006

Elm Park has lots to look forward to. The brand new "green" library, unique in London, is a real symbol of a new age and the planned new primary school will hopefully match the needs of a twenty first century community. Clubs and societies thrive from bowls and choral singing to stamp collecting and art. The Assembly Hall hosts a multitude of groups and the various church halls all provide space for Elm Park residents to meet and share their interests.

No longer the rural countryside which greeted the first residents, Elm Park is still surrounded by green spaces. Harrow Lodge Park in the north is complemented by The Chase running alongside the Beam and Hornchurch Country Park is to the east. On the old airfield there are major plans for a Visitor Centre, expected to open in 2011, completing the transformation of the wartime airbase to a haven for nature and history.

By 2001 there were 12,048 people living in Elm Park in 4,995 households, not a city, but a small town, which has grown and established its own identity, from the 300 houses built by 1935. We hope Elm Park residents past, present and future enjoy this story of Elm Park's first 75 years - a place with a unique history.

An established community from the air, the boating lake in Harrow Lodge Park is visible and Abbs Cross School is in the foreground. 1991

Modern postcard of Elm Park.

BIBLIOGRAPHY

This is not an exhaustive bibliography but includes the key texts consulted in the preparation of this book.

BENTON, Tony
The Changing Face of Hornchurch
Sutton Publishing
0 75092039 4
1999

BROWNE, Douglas Gordon and
TULLETT, Keith
Bernard Spilsbury: his life and cases
Harper Collins
0586055746
1982

BULL, Eric editor
Elm Park: a brief history
1987

BYGRAVES, Max
In His Own Words
Breedon Books Publishing Company
1 85983 079X
1997

CLARK, A.P.
Ecce Saceros Magnus
1977

CORBETT, Ronnie
High Hopes
Random House
0091873819
2000

COSTAIN, Sir Albert
Reflections
New Wellington Press
0 951264303
1987

DONNELLY, Paul
Essex Murders
Wharncliffe Books
1845630378
2007

FULCHER, Roger G. and
GUSTARD, Alan
Geography of Rainham - Thesis
1966

GREENWOOD, Pamela, PERRING,
Dominic and ROWSOME, Peter
From Ice Age To Essex: a history of the people and landscape of East London
Museum of London Archaeology Service
1 901 992 616
2006

HART, Douglas E.
Report of the surveyor ... on the parks and recreation grounds owned by the Council and as to contemplated improvements and expenditure in connection therewith.
Hornchurch Urban District Council
1937

HOLDEN'S Annual London and County Directory
1811

HORNCHURCH URBAN DISTRICT COUNCIL
Official Guides 1953-1964/5

HORNCHURCH URBAN DISTRICT COUNCIL
Council Diaries 1938 – 1964/5

HORNCHURCH URBAN DISTRICT COUNCIL
Minutes 1930-1965

JACKSON, Alan
Semi-detached London
Wild Swan Publications
1 874103011
2nd revised edition 1991

KELLY'S DIRECTORY
1878-1937
LEWIS, Frank
A History of Rainham with Wennington and South Hornchurch
Peter R. Davis
1966

LONDON BOROUGH OF HAVERING
Official Guides 1965 onwards

LONDON BOROUGH OF HAVERING YOUNG PEOPLE'S LIBRARY SERVICE
Elm Park Local History Infopack
London Borough of Havering
1992

LYSONS, Daniel
Handbook to the environs of London
1796

MORANT, Philip
The history and antiquities of the County of Essex compiled from the best and most ancient historians from Domesday book...2 volumes.
1768

OGBORNE, Elizabeth
The history of Essex from the earliest period to the present time.
1814

HORNCHURCH COUNTRY PARK
London Borough of Havering Historic Environment Study and Management Plan: 3 volumes
Oxford Archaeology
March 2008

PERFECT, Charles Thomas
Hornchurch During The Great War
Benham and Company Ltd.
1920

PERFECT, Charles Thomas
Ye Olde Village of Hornchurch
Benham and Company Ltd.
1917

PICGOT AND CO's DIRECTORY OF ESSEX
1832

PORTER, Sydney
London Borough of Havering Brochure on Parks and Recreation Grounds
London Borough of Havering
March 1966

PORTER, Sydney
Hornchurch Urban District Council Report on Parks and Recreations Grounds
Hornchurch Urban District Council
September 1961

POST OFFICE DIRECTORY
1855 and 1859

POWELL, W.R. editor
Essex Volume 7
Victoria History of the Counties of England
Oxford University Press
1978

RENTON, Peter
Lost Synagogues of London
Tymsder Publishing
0953110478
2nd Revised edition 2004

RICE, Ian
The Elm Park Estate, Hornchurch: a glimpse of the 1930s sales pitch
Twentieth Century Society Magazine
Spring 2008 pp 14-15

SALMON, Nathaniel
The history and antiquities of Essex
1740-42

SMITH, Eric
First Things First RAF Hornchurch and RAF Suttons Farm 1915-1962
Ian Henry Publications
0 860254429
1992

SMITH, Harold
*History of the Parish of
Havering-atte-Bower, Essex*
Benham and Company Ltd
1925

SMITH, Richard C.
*Hornchurch Scramble: the
definitive account of the RAF
Fighter Airfield, its pilots,
groundcrew and staff.Volume 1
1915 to the end of the Battle of
Britain*
Grub Street
1902304624
2000

SMITH, Richard C.
*Hornchurch Offensive: the
definitive account of the RAF
Fighter Airfield, its pilots,
groundcrew and staff.Volume 2
1941 to the airfield's final closure.*
Grub Street
1902304799
2001

SMITH, Richard C.
*Second to none: a pictorial
Hornchurch Aerodrome through
two world wars and beyond, 1915-
1962*
Grub Street
1904010784
2004

STRATMANN, Linda
Essex Murders
Sutton Books
0750935545
2004

SUTTON, Squadron Leader H.T.
Sutton OBE DFC
*Raiders Approach: the fighter
tradition of RAF Station
Hornchurch and Sutton's Farm*
Gale and Folden Limited
1956

TOTTERDELL, G.H.
Country Copper
George Harrap and Co. Ltd.

WATT, Peter
Hitler v Havering
Carlton Armitage Press
0 95240320X
1994

*WHITE'S History, Gazeteer and
Directory of the County of Essex*
1848 and 1863

WITARD, Doris
*Bibles In Barrels: a history of
Essex Baptists*
Essex Baptist Association
1962

WRIGHT, Thomas
*The history and topography of the
county of Essex*
1836

NEWSPAPERS

*Hornchurch and Upminster Echo
Hornchurch and Upminster News
Romford Recorder
Romford Times*

INDEX